I MANIFESTED MY WORST NIGHTMARE

ABIGAIL E. MYATT

I MANIFESTED MY WORST NIGHTMARE

How Jesus Rescued Mc from New Age Lies

I MANIFESTED MY WORST NIGHTMARE
How Jesus Rescued Me from New Age Lies

Copyright © 2025 by Abigail E. Myatt

All Scripture quotations, unless otherwise indicated, are taken from The Holy Bible, New International Version®, NIV®. Copyright ©1973, 1978, 1984, 2011 by Biblica, Inc. Used by permission of Zondervan. All rights reserved worldwide.

Scripture quotations marked (NLT) are taken from the Holy Bible, New Living Translation, copyright ©1996, 2004, 2015 by Tyndale House Foundation. Used by permission of Tyndale House Publishers, Carol Stream, Illinois 60188. All rights reserved.

Scripture quotations marked (NKJV) are taken from the New King James Version®. Copyright © 1982 by Thomas Nelson. Used by permission. All rights reserved.

Disclaimer: For privacy reasons, some names, locations, and dates may have been changed. This book deals honestly with mature themes and is best suited for older teens and adults. It has been published for the purpose of providing the reader with general information on its subject matter. The author and the publisher believe the information to be accurate and authoritative at the time of publication. The book is sold with the understanding that neither the author nor the publisher is providing professional advice, and the reader should not rely upon this book as such. Every situation is different, and professional advice (whether psychological, legal, financial, tax, or otherwise) should only be obtained from a professional licensed in your jurisdiction who has knowledge of the specific facts and circumstances.

Book Cover Design by Jaclynn Braden
Cover illustration by Abigail Myatt
Interior Layout and Design by Stephanie Anderson
Editorial Team: Traci Matt, Jamie Smith, Sara Brunsvold, Rachel Maier

ISBNs:
979-8-89165-359-7 *Paperback*
979-8-89165-360-3 *Hardback*
979-8-89165-358-0 *E-book*

Published by:
Streamline Books
Kansas City, MO
shareyourstory.com

To my husband, Josiah.
Without you, no one would be reading this right now.
Thank you for your love, support, and
unwavering belief in me and this story.

CONTENTS

FOREWORD

When I first picked up Abigail's book, I felt like I was reading pages torn straight out of my own story. Her words carried me back to the years I spent searching for worth in unhealthy relationships, attention-seeking, and counterfeit healing practices. Like Abigail, I walked the path of deception, trying everything to fix my brokenness except turning to the only one who could truly heal me: Jesus Christ.

That's why this book matters so much. Abigail doesn't just tell her story; she gives language to the silent struggles many of us have lived but never dared to speak aloud. Each chapter draws you in with raw honesty and leaves you eager to know where her path on the dark side led, how she escaped the ungodly relationships, and what it finally took for her to heal.

She shines light on hidden wounds—the shame, the desperate attempts to feel loved, the lure of New Age promises—that so many quietly carry. And she does it in a way that makes you feel less alone. For those who have endured the unthinkable, from occult practices to selling your body just to survive, Abigail's story doesn't only echo your pain, it walks you toward redemption.

I had countless moments of uncomfortable recognition while reading. Cringeworthy reflections where I thought, "Yes, that was me too." Yet instead of leaving us in that pain, Abigail reminds us that we are not defined by the darkness we once embraced. She points us to the truth that no matter how the enemy has tried to destroy us, God is able to pick up every broken piece and put us back together more whole, more holy, and more beautiful than we ever imagined.

And Abigail doesn't stop with her testimony. The appendices are gifts in themselves. With clarity and conviction, she unmasks the appealing language of New Age spirituality—terms the world has embraced as normal—and replaces them with the timeless truth of Scripture. In doing so, she not only shares her journey but also equips readers with discernment and direction.

If you've ever felt lost in shame, trapped in cycles of deception, or empty from chasing meaning in all the wrong places, you will find yourself in these pages. More importantly, you will find hope—the hope that Christ redeems, restores, and heals even the worst of our nightmares.

This book will reach both seekers and skeptics alike, speaking to the heart through Abigail's lived experience and to the mind through her clear and constructive teaching.

It is my honor to commend this book to you. Read it with openness. Let it convict and comfort you. And may it draw you nearer to the only true source of healing and freedom: our Lord and Savior, Jesus Christ.

Michaela Nikolaenko
Host of the *Raised & Redeemed* Podcast

PART 1
LOST IN THE WORLD

NOWHERE LEFT TO RUN

I never could have imagined that one day I'd call Jesus my savior.

Not when I was casting spells.

Not when I was tripping on psychedelics.

Definitely not when I was naked on camera, convinced I was reclaiming my power.

I prided myself on my unique way of seeing the world. One that never included Jesus. Pride? Arrogance? Reckless decisions fueled by unmanaged mental illness? Absolutely. But Jesus? That was crazy talk.

I wanted meaning, success, and fulfillment, but instead, I found darkness, shame, and guilt. I searched for healing but kept reopening old wounds. I chased freedom but became more enslaved. I followed what I thought was light, spiritual awakenings, higher consciousness, divine feminine energy, only to find myself in the deepest pit I had ever known.

The world promised me enlightenment, but what I actually found was exactly what Paul warns about in Galatians 5:19–21: the obvious works of the flesh, which refer to the destructive impulses that come from our human nature when we live apart from God. Things like sexual immorality, selfish ambition, envy, hatred, strife, drunkenness, and other harmful characteristics. I saw all of it firsthand in the underbelly of Hollywood. Sexual immorality paraded as empowerment, impurity disguised as self-expression, lustful pleasures masquerading as self-love. I was surrounded by idolatry, worshiping success, money, and myself. I dabbled in sorcery through psychedelics, manifestation, and tarot cards, blind to the demonic doors I was opening. I saw the destruction caused by hostility, jealousy, and selfish ambition, the way people tore each other apart for a taste of fame. I witnessed drunkenness and wild parties, where lost souls numbed their emptiness with substances and temporary highs. It was all dressed up as a glamorous life, but underneath it was nothing but bondage.

Not because I was a monster, but because I was a sinner. And I wasn't ready to accept that I needed a savior.

Humans are made to worship. Think about it. Whether it's money, celebrities, a certain lifestyle, the universe, vibes, atheism, science, or even ourselves. We all bow to something. And since my deep-seated childhood wounds went unaddressed for most of my life, I worshiped everything but God.

I worshiped myself.

I worshiped the world.

And eventually, I worshiped the sparkly, cutesy aesthetic of the New Age: yoga, crystals, psychics, witches, tarot, astrology.

Manifestation—the seductive promise everyone is chasing.

It all looked like light, but in reality, it was a hollow glow masking deep and dangerous darkness.

My heart was hardened against Jesus. He had no place in my life. I didn't just reject him, I ran in the opposite direction, convinced I knew better. No matter how many warnings I ignored, no matter how many times I fell flat on my face, I refused to see the truth. I was blind, but I called it enlightenment. I was deceived, but I called it freedom. I was lost, but I convinced myself I was in control.

I chased everything he warned against and suffered the consequences of my own choices. And yet, despite how deep I fell, how many stones I hit on my way to rock bottom, how much I rejected him, when I had nowhere left to run, he was there.

No Boundaries

I was lying in the bathtub, squinting at the faucet, convinced there were cameras hidden inside. Convinced my life was being broadcast on live television for the world to see. Maybe it was the weed or the paranoia that crept in after years of experimenting with psychedelics, tarot, manifestation, and other spiritual practices that I thought were harmless but were actually an invitation for spiritual darkness to take hold of my life. Maybe it was the spiraling effects of my bipolar disorder, which had become so overwhelming that I was like a schizophrenic being tormented by delusions.

Or maybe it was something buried deeper—the trauma of growing up without boundaries, of never feeling truly safe or seen. Privacy didn't exist in our home. Doors didn't stay closed for long, and emotions were often exposed rather than protected. I learned early that my inner world wasn't my own, and that sense of a lack of safety followed me into adulthood.

There were no locks on our doors. No boundaries. Nothing in my life felt protected. That constant sense of being watched and invaded stuck with me. And the cycle continued.

For years, I opened doors to the unseen with my constant marijuana and psilocybin use. I surrounded myself with people who were no good for me, made bad decisions that only deepened my wounds. I gave my body away to men who had no intentions of marrying me, let alone respecting me.

But I was convinced I was on a special journey, convinced I was destined for greatness. Actress, singer, healer, I didn't know which one I would become, but I was certain the universe had my back, that I was following the path meant for me.

Still, no matter how many luxurious apartments I lived in, no matter how many beaches I sat on, no matter how many trips I took, the same feeling always returned. The grief of my own failure. The torment of never being enough—not successful enough, not admired enough, not enlightened enough.

I told myself I just needed to try harder. Learn more about my birth chart. Perfect my tarot readings. Meditate better. Manifest stronger. I was addicted to self-improvement, to the idea that if I could just fix myself, I would find peace. But no matter what I did, no matter how much I chased after perfection, I was never free. Jesus had no place in my heart. I had kicked him to the curb by fourth grade and didn't want to let him back in.

Until one day, I lost everything. Again. I found myself in a relationship where I was financially dependent on an older man. Again. Trading my body for survival. Again. I was consumed with shame, but I convinced myself it wasn't as bad as it seemed, that I was in control.

Then, at the end of the road, when there were no more detours, no more distractions, no more lies I could tell myself, I met Jesus. Not in a church. Not in a moment of religious curiosity. But when I had nowhere left to turn. I had hit the end of my rope. I couldn't go on. And in the darkness, he said: "You are mine." For the first time, I listened.

What truly surprised me, what I never saw coming, was that despite everything I had done, despite the mess I had made of my life, he was still there. He loved me. And that was the beginning of something completely new.

This book is about deception. How the world deceives us. How the New Age deceived me. How easy it is for a broken person to fall into the trap of false light. But most of all, this book is about Jesus.

My story is proof that no one is too far gone for him. No matter how lost, how broken, how ashamed we are, he is still waiting. Still ready to redeem, restore, and transform.

I had to face the truth about myself—the mistakes I made, the lies I believed. And while it wasn't easy, it was necessary. We all are only human, and we all have to be honest with ourselves if we want healing through the truth and through Jesus.

Not only did he rescue me, but he gave me everything I had been searching for: peace, protection, purpose. A family, a husband. He even made me a momma. He blessed me in ways I never could have imagined. Not because I deserved it, but because he is a good God.

Lies' Deep Roots

There is a rising tide of deception in today's culture—New Age spirituality, self-worship, moral relativism. So many people are searching for meaning, but they're being led down the same road I was, one that ends in darkness, confusion, and bondage. I wrote this book for the person who feels lost. The one searching for something real. The one who knows, deep down, that there must be more than this.

I spent years running from the truth. Hiding from my mistakes and my brokenness, believing the lies I told myself. But when I finally ran out of places to hide, I discovered that Jesus had been there all along, waiting, ready, and willing to save me.

This is the story of how I found the only one who could truly set me free, the one who offers not just freedom from the lies of the world, but healing, redemption, and a new life. And he's ready to offer the same to anyone who is willing to be honest with themselves and embrace the truth he provides.

But deception doesn't start the moment you fall for a lie; it begins long before that. It's planted like a seed, buried deep in moments we don't fully understand until much later.

Looking back, I can see now that the road I walked was paved long before I ever stepped onto it. The longing, the searching, the wounds that made me so susceptible to the lies of the world didn't start in adulthood. They started in my childhood, in the house I grew up in, in the things that were said to me and the things that were never said at all.

Before I ever cast a spell or turned over a tarot card, before I ever sought validation from men or numbed myself with alcohol, I was just a little girl trying to find her place in a chaotic world. A little girl who craved love, safety, and belonging but instead, found confusion, pain, and an ache she couldn't name.

And so, to truly understand my story, we have to go back to the beginning.

CHAPTER 1

NOT MEANT TO BE LOVED

ife had felt off for a while, but it wasn't the first time. That uneasy feeling in my stomach was all too familiar, the kind that makes you jittery and sends you running to the bathroom. I'd felt it as a kid walking into gymnastics practice, unsure if I'd stick my tumbling pass or slam down on my already-bruised tailbone. I felt it when I was called on to read in class, squinting at a board I couldn't see clearly because I needed glasses. But worst of all, I felt it at home, waiting, always waiting, for something to go wrong.

One particular day in 2003 stands out. My mom hadn't been herself for months, which, in our house, usually meant one thing. My dad gathered me and my four siblings in the living room, grinning as he announced that our mom was having another baby. I couldn't tell if he thought it was good news or bad. He didn't hide the fact that she was depressed, and now there would be six of us kids. I remember wondering why this kept happening when they were always fighting about money. I didn't realize then but this cycle would repeat itself four more times before I left for college—ten kids before the divorce.

I remember in fourth grade when I went to a friend's house and saw her parents having a normal conversation, one that didn't involve insults, shouting, or resentment. I think I even saw them . . . hug?! I thought, *Is this what love is supposed to look like?* Because I had never seen my parents interact that way. The chaos at home shaped my understanding of love, security, and what it meant to feel safe, or, more accurately, the absence of those things. I spent a lot of time with her family to avoid my home. I would eat dinner with them most nights. I don't think anyone in my family noticed I was gone.

Home Sweet Home

Home had a smell: baby soap, faintly sour milk, something always cooking on the stove. It sounded like crying, arguing, toys clattering against the floor, basketballs being thrown against the wall, and the muffled noise of a TV left on too long. There were crumbs on the couch cushions, and the carpet needed to be vacuumed. It felt familiar because it was all I knew, but often, it felt like a place I needed to run from.

Growing up, I always felt a tension that wrapped around me like a shadow, something I couldn't name but could never escape. I learned early that love was unpredictable, that it could be warm one moment and withdrawn the next, like a door that slammed shut without warning. My feelings didn't seem to matter. I learned to shrink, to disappear, to become whatever I needed to be to avoid rejection or anger.

In my family, comfort and emotional support weren't things we knew how to give. Instead, teasing, name-calling, and humiliation were common. My parents weren't a united front, and it showed. Rather than being on the same team, they often felt like opponents arguing, undermining each other, and speaking badly about one another behind closed doors. The good that came from their marriage was ten beautiful children, but for me, there was also a lot of pain. It was confusing to feel caught in the middle, unsure whose version of reality to trust and feeling pressured to take sides. Sadly, some of those dynamics still linger even more than a decade after their divorce.

I learned early that love was unpredictable, that it could be warm one moment and withdrawn the next, like a door that slammed shut without warning.

There's a particular kind of confusion that comes with family dysfunction. It doesn't leave bruises, but it marks you just the same. I became the peacemaker, the absorber of tension, the one who believed love had to be earned. I either felt too much or not enough, and neither felt safe. I didn't know back then that the shame I carried wasn't mine to bear. As a child, I only knew how to hold it.

I walked through life with invisible wounds, trying to make sense of things I couldn't put into words. In the silence, I convinced myself that maybe I wasn't meant to be loved in the way I longed for. Maybe I wasn't meant to be protected the way a child should be. It took years for me to see the truth that love isn't supposed to feel like that. But back then, it was all I knew.

My dad wasn't like other dads. He went ding-dong-ditching with us, took us on vacations, and once taught me how to do a roundoff back handspring in the backyard. He'd sneak us onto private property just so we could explore houses in the middle of construction. Rules didn't seem to apply to him.

Sometimes that made me uneasy, but other times, I loved the sense of adventure it brought. He could be the "cool dad," and I never quite knew which side of that coin he'd land on in any given moment.

My mom wasn't a touchy-feely person, and she wasn't one to offer compliments or encouragement. But her presence made me feel safe. She was my steady place, my comfort. I didn't always get the attention I longed for from her, but I never doubted that she loved me the best she could.

Growing up in a big family shaped my identity in ways I didn't realize until much later. With each new baby, the attention I once had dwindled. I became a pro at changing diapers and mediating fights between toddlers. My parents fought constantly, mostly about money, and I found myself hoarding things for comfort. Whenever my mom took me shopping, I would push for as much as I could get, desperate to fit in. In fifth grade, I wouldn't leave my house unless my outfit had an Abercrombie moose logo somewhere on it. I learned to place my worth in material things, to seek validation outside my home because I wasn't getting it inside. This need for affirmation made me vulnerable to manipulation from friends, men, or anyone who seemed to offer the love and security and attention I lacked.

As a little girl, I loved to sing. I would quietly hum along to songs in the car or around the house, matching pitch effortlessly, feeling alive in those small moments. But that joy didn't last. Family members would tell me to stop, would tell me that I was bad at singing, or simply ignore my voice. Over time, I started to believe them, and with that, a little piece of me went silent. I began to hold back in class, too. Even when I knew the answer, I'd shrink into my seat, afraid to speak up. My dad often told me that I was selfish, I just wanted attention, or I was a bad person. I can see now that much of it was his own pain and projection, but as a child, I absorbed it as truth. His voice became my inner voice, echoing in my mind long after the words were spoken. Somewhere along the way, I learned that my voice could be controlled—or silenced—by others, and I carried that lesson far into my adult life.

Search for Identity

Religion wasn't a big part of my childhood. My mom had some faith in Christ, but my dad wouldn't let her teach us about Jesus. The Catholic church we occasionally attended was painfully boring, and the hour-long service dragged on like it would never end. I definitely couldn't relate to anything I heard or saw. Church became a thing of the past. My maternal Christian grandparents would tell me about God, but my dad would scoff and list all the reasons why their beliefs were ridiculous. He talked about evolution, about science, about the lies Christians told themselves to feel better. There was an impact in his words that I didn't fully understand back then—a bitterness that, looking back, seemed to come from a deep, personal, painful place. By fourth grade, I had made up my mind: God wasn't real. I even told my friends how foolish it was to believe in him. It became like a mission for me to save them from ignorance.

Without faith, I searched for my identity elsewhere. I quit gymnastics in eighth grade, exhausted by its demands on my body, mind, and social life. I practiced for more than twenty hours a week, and the constant strain left me with injuries in my tailbone, back, knees, and elbows, making the toll even heavier. Leaving something that had consumed so much of my time and energy left me unmoored, longing for control in a chaotic world. As I neared the end of middle school, I shifted my focus to popularity. Little did I know I would gain social status in high school but lose even more of myself in the process.

My freshman year of high school, I joined the cheer team and made new friends. I got my braces off and felt beautiful for the first time. But even as my confidence grew outwardly, I still felt empty inside. Then, when I saw photos online of the popular kids drinking during the homecoming dance afterparty my friends and I weren't invited to, I immediately started planning. We needed to get drunk. Yesterday.

That weekend, we raided my friend's parents' liquor cabinet. We took turns trying different drinks, each one burning worse than the last. That first night, I didn't actually get drunk, but I pretended to be. Soon, we were drinking every weekend in my friend's basement. I still remember the first time I got so sick I spent an entire day throwing up. You'd think that would have deterred me, but it didn't. I was still searching for escape, for belonging, for something to fill the void. Sadly, I thought I would only be fun to be around if I wasn't myself.

Looking back now, I see how much childhood pain shaped my understanding of love, security, and self-worth. But pain is not our identity. God was there, even in those moments, even when I couldn't see him. "The Lord is close to the brokenhearted and saves those who are crushed in spirit" (Psalm 34:18). Though I didn't know it then, he was already writing my story of redemption.

I didn't have words for it at the time, but something in my childhood left me unsettled. The emotional undercurrents, confusion, and shame I carried all left me feeling unsafe in my own home. I couldn't explain why; I just knew that safety and trust felt foreign to me. And I knew I didn't believe in God.

That was the one lesson my dad made sure I learned. There was no higher power watching over me, no divine plan, no purpose beyond what science could explain. He was so sure of it that I became sure, too. I clung to atheism like a shield, rejecting anything that resembled faith.

But rejection doesn't fill a void; it only deepens it.

CHAPTER 2

PRETTY, POPULAR, AND EMPTY

Everyone in our town knew the Nelson sisters. They had money, a big house, and a dad who could intimidate anyone in a courtroom. Even in elementary school, they had a kind of untouchable status. And Mr. Nelson? He was the kind of man you didn't cross. But to me, he was something else too—off.

Steph Nelson and I weren't exactly best friends, but we were always in each other's orbit. We had history. We had competition. We had moments of forced closeness, like being on the cheer team together, but there was always something simmering underneath. She needed all eyes on her. She didn't like being outshined. And if I liked a boy, she had to have him.

Our rivalry started in third-grade gymnastics. We had been teammates, and even then, there was an unspoken contest between us of who could be the best, the strongest, the most admired. I started excelling beyond her, and eventually, she quit. But she didn't quit the competition. Instead, she just changed the game.

Steph ruled the social scene. She had the parties, the influence, and a carefully cultivated group of friends who cycled through phases of excluding and bullying each other in an endless game of power. I had my own close friends, Emma and Lily, and we kept out of the drama and focused on our dorky accents and facial expressions in our own little world, but Steph always managed to insert herself into my life at just the right times. I'd let her, partly because it was easier, and partly because I wanted to be wanted. Emma and Lily would belt out in song together, and I would watch them, unable to join in. Something was physically making me stop. I was too afraid to hit notes or that my voice would crack. All I wanted was to be free like them.

Then there was Oliver, my first real boyfriend. He was sweet, funny, and I really liked him. But Steph liked the fact that I liked him even more. She didn't even hide it. First, she planted the seeds, telling me Oliver was planning to break up with me. Then she told him I was planning to break up with him. Next thing I knew, they were together. Just like that.

But somehow, I stayed friends with her. Maybe I was used to the bully dynamic. Maybe I believed that friendships were supposed to come with a side of betrayal. Maybe I was just afraid of being on the outside.

Mr. Nelson

Steph's house became a frequent backdrop to my high school experience. It was the place to be—the parties, the gossip, the carefully maintained hierarchy of who was in and who was out. And every time I went over, I felt Mr. Nelson's presence. Not just because he was there, but because he noticed me.

Mr. Nelson was intense. Everyone knew him as a powerhouse lawyer, the kind of man who could tear you apart with a single look. But when I came over to their house, he wasn't intimidating.

He was nice . . . too nice. His compliments were too much, his attention too focused.

"Abby, you're the prettiest girl in the whole school. You'll be homecoming queen one day," he'd say, his voice dripping with a strange kind of certainty. I'd laugh it off, but even then, something about it made my stomach twist.

At first, I brushed off all his attention as simply a dad trying to be nice. But as I got older, the compliments never stopped, and they felt more intentional. It was uncomfortable, but in a way, it also felt like validation. The whole world around me reinforced that my worth was in how much attention I got, and him noticing me was just another example.

My house was chaos. My mom was constantly pregnant, and I kept it a secret, terrified that if the popular girls found out, they'd think I was weird. The truth was, I hated how crowded and loud it was at home. There was always fighting, always something dramatic happening, and with so many siblings, I learned how to slip under the radar. I spent as much time out of the house as possible. If I could be anywhere but there, I would be. Looking back, I was probably starting to come off as desperate to my peers.

First Heartbreak

When I started drinking, I never thought it would become an issue. I thought only stupid people became alcoholics, and I was smart—honor roll, pre-med aspirations, the whole thing. Drinking was just another way to be social, another way to fit in. But even then, there were signs that I ignored.

I started experimenting early on in drunken states. I somehow was always drunkenly making out with my girlfriends. I didn't think much of it. I clearly liked boys when I was sober. But they kept hurting me. I felt like I was being used.

High school was a strange mix of craving acceptance and feeling completely out of place. It set the foundation for so many of the choices I would make later, choices that would take me down darker roads than I ever imagined.

There was a boy in my English class named Rob. He wasn't my typical type, but I tended to go for personality. He made me laugh so hard with his different accents and bits that I would look forward to English class just to see him. We started dating, and he began gaining popularity, too.

Steph and Emma were dating older boys. They would exchange stories about how they lost their virginities, and suddenly, my virginity didn't seem like anything sacred. It was just last season's Hollister graphic tee that needed to be discarded.

On one of our weekly weekend benders in Steph's basement, we snuck Rob over, and I had sex with him in her twin sister's bed. It was nothing groundbreaking. I didn't feel any connection, partly because I was under the influence and partly because I probably disassociated.

I was under the impression that we were both virgins. Then, months later, I found out he had slept with a girl on my cheer team before we started dating. I freaked out—not because he did it, but because he didn't tell me. I called them both disgusting, and from that point on, everything slowly unraveled until he eventually dumped me over text. I made him come over and do it in person and basically begged him not to.

I was completely wrecked. Partly because I felt emotionally attached to him and had given him something I couldn't get back, and partly because, while I had broken up with boys before, a boy had never broken up with me, and my inflated ego was badly destroyed.

I suffered in silence because I was too embarrassed to tell my friends what really happened. "It was mutual," I told Emma and Lily. But I think they knew I was lying.

I lost fifteen pounds off my already slender build and couldn't get Rob out of my head. Every time my phone went off, I hoped and prayed to the God I didn't believe in that it was him.

Finally, after the longest summer of my life, he asked me to get back together the first week of senior year. I accepted immediately—pathetic, I know—only for him to dump me a few days later. Again. Was he trying to ruin me?

He had elevated his social status so much that every morning of my senior year, I would walk up the main steps of the school and see him sitting with my group of friends before first period. You can't make this up.

I slept with a few other guys at my school to try to forget about it all, unknowingly giving away more and more of myself, my self-respect, and my soul. Slowly ruining my reputation. Ironically, I carefully crafted my image on social media.

Finally, at the end of senior year, I got over him. And luckily for my ego, my first year at Michigan State University, he and I both ended up at the same party, and he drunkenly begged for me back. I can't lie—it was one of the highlights of my life at that point, especially because I was already dating someone else.

Best Friend Betrayals

Rob wasn't the only person who betrayed me during senior year. Steph Nelson grew more seriously fed up as the time for selecting fall homecoming court neared. Every time someone mentioned they were voting for me—or maybe it was her dad's inability to keep his mouth shut about it—I felt her rage. I knew

I was in the danger zone. Funny part is that neither of us even made the court.

Steph was working overtime to turn my friends against me. She convinced Lily that my prom dress was copying hers even though every other girl in school had a slightly different version of the same brightly colored strapless dress with bedazzled top. They didn't even include me in their prom group because my date wasn't in their friend group.

Then Lily's graduation party happened. That's when everything really blew up.

What time should I get there to help set up? I texted Lily, my closest friend since fourth grade, the one who knew my darkest thoughts, the one I used to confide in.

Oh, just come when it starts, it's fine!

That was weird. I knew my other friends were going early to help. My stomach clenched, but I brushed it off. Maybe I was overthinking.

When I arrived at the party, Lily led me to her bedroom to drop off my things. That's when I noticed it. Steph's phone, plugged into the charger. My heart tensed. Something felt off. All night, they barely acknowledged me, their conversations shifting the moment I approached. Their smiles were thin, their laughs forced.

After a few drinks, liquid courage took over. I slipped into Lily's bedroom, my pulse hammering in my ears. My fingers hesitated over Steph's phone before unlocking it. I navigated to her texts, my breath quickening.

I typed my name into the search bar.

Omg Abby wants to be invited up north so bad.

She's so annoying.

I felt like I had been punched in the gut. My stomach churned. Heat flooded my face as I read the messages over and over, as if the words might change. But they didn't. These were the girls I had poured my energy into. The ones I had built my high school world around. And this is what they thought of me. Rage swallowed the sadness before I could even process it. I walked out of that room knowing I was done. *Bye.*

It hurt, of course. But I refused to give them the satisfaction of seeing it. I had other acquaintances to fall back on. I moved on, at least on the surface. A year later, Lily admitted to me, "I was jealous of you. I'm sorry." Steph never did. None of the others did. A moment like that should roll off your back in high school. People grow apart. Drama happens. But it didn't roll off mine. It cemented something deep inside me—that friendships weren't safe. Maybe I wasn't built for them. Maybe I was the problem.

That night, and so many moments before and after, made me question my ability to form real, lasting relationships with other women. I told myself I just *didn't get along* with girls. I wasn't catty enough, wasn't dramatic enough, didn't possess whatever secret ingredient it took to stay close without getting burned.

> It cemented something deep inside me—that friendships weren't safe. Maybe I wasn't built for them. Maybe I was the problem.

I had spent years carefully building a friend group, girls I thought would always be there, only to end up on the outside, looking in. I was left questioning why I had even cared so much in the first place. Why had I spent so much energy curating my social life and my image when, in the end, none of it mattered?

For years, I was convinced that my inability to maintain friendships meant there was something fundamentally wrong with me.

I genuinely believed that I lacked some unknown rulebook on how to be a friend.

It wasn't until I met Jesus that I understood the truth.

I wasn't incapable of friendships. I just wasn't meant for shallow, performative relationships based on gossip, competition, and alcohol-fueled memories. I was meant for genuine friendships, rooted in truth, accountability, and love.

And I found them.

When I gave my life to Christ, I became a better friend. I learned what it meant to love people without needing something in return. I also learned that not everyone deserved access to me. Now, my circle is small. And it's better that way.

Two other major things happened in my childhood household during my senior year of high school. My mom gave birth to my little brother and her tenth child, andddd my parents divorced. Oh, and my dad started dating a woman twenty years his junior. It was all messy. I couldn't wait to get away.

College was supposed to be a fresh start, but instead, it became a freefall. Without my parents' already disinterested eyes on me, without rules or limits, I dove headfirst into the party scene. What started as weekend drinking in high school became my entire identity. And if I thought I had given pieces of myself away before, I had no idea what was coming next.

CHAPTER 3

VODKA, VALIDATION, AND YOGA

"**H**urry up, Abby, we're going to Piiiiiikkkkkkeeeee!" My sorority sisters couldn't contain their excitement that THE coolest fraternity chose us to invite over for their last-minute snow day party.

I sat in front of my mirror, digging into my lacey makeup bag, rummaging past eyeliner pencil shavings. *I know I stashed one in here. Yep, there it is.* I secretly pulled out three little red-and-blue pills. Lyrica. A muscle relaxer meant for old people with joint pain, but I knew a psychiatrist in training who introduced me to its other effects. It practically erased anxiety and made you feel like you were floating. While it did cause me to slur my words a little and turned my stomach into a bottomless pit, making me eat everything in sight and contributing to my rapid college weight gain, it made me talkative and carefree.

I washed the pills down with the raspberry Smirnoff hidden in my water bottle, adjusted my black Alpha Phi beanie, pulled my oversized crewneck over my leggings, and slipped into my Adidas Superstars. "Readyyyy!"

What a sight to behold we were, a group of twenty sorority girls walking in minus-ten-degree weather without coats singing "Timber" by Ke$ha. Nothing but the vodka keeping us warm. The second we walked into the fraternity house, the smell of beer, sweat, and cheap cologne hit me. Fraternity houses all had the same distinct scent. The music pounded so hard I could feel it vibrating in my chest.

It never ceased to amaze me that these boys ignored me like I didn't exist. Maybe they all took a class on how to make girls feel invisible until they're desperate enough to sleep with them. *I'm not drunk enough.* I chased down as much vodka as I could, hoping maybe my fun side would come out.

Unhinged

But instead of wiping the board clean, I just kept scribbling over the mess, layering bad decisions on top of each other like thick, black marker strokes.

College was my chance to reinvent myself, or so I thought. It was supposed to be the fresh start I needed, a clean slate, a place where I could finally be someone worthy and be away from my dysfunctional family. But instead of wiping the board clean, I just kept scribbling over the mess, layering bad decisions on top of each other like thick, black marker strokes.

Without my family around, I had nothing tethering me to reality. My new "family" became sorority sisters who barely knew me and less-than-average frat boys I was desperate to impress. My two priorities were keeping up my grades and proving I was the kind of girl who could shotgun a beer faster than anyone in the room. I wanted to be effortless—the straight-A student who could also throw back shots like one of the guys.

But it wasn't effortless. It was exhausting.

I woke up the day after the snow-day party confused and anxious in my bed. *How did I get here? Whatever.* At least I hadn't woken up in some random dude's room with sticky floors and the stench of beer and body odor, which unfortunately had happened before. I blocked out the multiple assaults. It's like I somehow thought they were normal.

I squinted at my phone. *Crap.* My physiology exam was the next day.

I pulled myself up, feeling like my brain was misfiring, the neurons sluggish and slow. *Need. Adderall.* Good thing I had one. I didn't bother with breakfast. Adderall killed my appetite, so I took the opportunity to put myself into a little "calorie deficit," you could say. For the next eight hours, I would be hyper-focused, hands shaking, mind racing. And when I needed to come down, I had a Xanax and a pre-roll of weed waiting.

I aced the test, of course. And voila, that's how it was done. I left out the part where, after hours of suppressing my appetite, I devoured an entire order of HopCat's fries with beer cheese during happy hour. The vodka sodas washed them down nicely. The alcohol would help free my voice and my inhibitions, which is part of the reason I gravitated toward it, but it wasn't true freedom. It was counterfeit, and it kept me in bondage.

I was constantly trying to control the highs and lows, and my body was paying the price. The drinking led to binge eating, and the binge eating led to weight gain—twenty-five pounds, to be exact. Some nights, I would stand in front of the mirror, staring at my bloated stomach, sucking it in as hard as I could, twisting my body to find an angle that made me look smaller. Other nights, I refused to look at all.

I hated myself. And when I hated myself, I drank more.

I got tired of being broke. My dad had withdrawn his financial support without warning, something that left me anxious and scrambling to stay afloat, so I had to take out loans and apply for grants. I was so incredibly clueless about all things financial, which only made it harder. I often felt jealous of my girlfriends whose dads made them feel safe and supported. My dad did a lot to provide for me, but I never felt fully safe, and sometimes I worried I'd end up on the streets. The stress of money weighed on me, but there was an easy fix: bartending. At least I'd get paid to be in the environment I practically lived in anyway.

Bartending Crash Course

I had never worked in the service industry before, but my Greek life connections (and looks) got me promoted to bartender immediately. It wasn't long before I realized I was in over my head. The industry was cutthroat. My coworkers, most of whom were older, seasoned servers who had been working there for years, weren't exactly welcoming. They smelled blood in the water. I was young, inexperienced, and suddenly making just as much in tips as they were.

But I had a protector: my forty-four-year-old bar manager.

He let me hit his vape whenever I wanted, made sure I got the best shifts, and, eventually, started inviting me to his apartment after work. We would get high and watch shows, and occasionally, we hooked up. But mostly, I just liked being around him. It felt like he was taking care of me in a way.

With him on my side, I got away with a lot. Even though there were cameras everywhere, I knew I could pocket extra cash from tips without consequence. He would never rat me out. At the time, I thought I had earned it. After all, I was bringing in my sorority and fraternity friends. Wasn't that worth something?

The cycle continued: drinking, drugs, validation, regret. I slept with more guys than I'd like to admit. Some of it I remember. Some of it I don't.

There was one moment, though, that stuck with me.

A coworker was on and off with a girl. He was a player, and he knew I was attracted to guys like him. One night, we hooked up. I didn't care if I was overstepping relationship bounds or if a guy was off-limits. The next day, while we were working the back bar together, he looked at me and, to my face, said, "Ugh, why can't you look like Taylor?"

Taylor was another one of our coworkers, and she was beautiful.

I didn't stand up for myself. I just laughed it off. My cheeks flushed, and I felt that pit in my stomach, the familiar pit from childhood. Why couldn't I be more beautiful? More desirable? More like Taylor?

And then, later that night, I slept with him again.

The self-destruction escalated.

Whatever guy I was fixated on at the moment would receive a hundred calls from me when I got drunk. I got ignored so many times. I was denied the one thing I craved. I was livid that these boys would lead me on, sleep with me, and then ignore me. I was being used! But were they the only ones doing the using? Or was I using them too? For attention, validation, love? I didn't even know what love was.

I was out of control. I thought I was going to take the hidden shame to my grave, but one night at a pregame, I snuck into the room of a guy who had flirted with me. A guy who had a girlfriend. I proceeded to take off all my clothes. My friends found me there and asked what in the world I was doing. I don't even remember it all. But the next day, I knew I had done something bad. My anxiety was almost heart-stopping.

One night, I crashed my moped—right in front of a cop. The pavement scraped my knee raw, blood pooling in the torn fabric of my leggings. My head swam, my pulse pounded, and I braced myself for the inevitable DUI. But somehow, miraculously, I got away with it. The cop followed me as I walked my moped home.

It should have been a wake-up call. It wasn't.

The next weekend, I was back at the bar, taking shots with my coworkers like nothing had happened, numbing that ever-present, gnawing ache inside me.

I would wake up crying in my bed almost every morning. I felt an impending doom with graduation approaching and the deadline to apply to med school coming closer, but I knew I didn't have it in me to go. The weight of it all pressed on my chest, suffocating me. I needed something to change.

I took action to get some relief. I scheduled an appointment and got diagnosed with bipolar II disorder. The doctor prescribed mood stabilizers, but I didn't put much thought into it. I swallowed the pills with alcohol. They dulled the edges, but they didn't stop me from spiraling. I didn't take my diagnosis seriously, instead considering it just something I needed to tough out. God forbid I accepted that I had a legitimate issue that needed to be addressed.

I was trapped in a loop, running full speed toward destruction and unable to hit the brakes.

By senior year, I was sick of it all. Sick of the parties, sick of hating my body, sick of chasing validation from people who didn't care about me. But I didn't know how to stop. I was trapped in a loop, running full speed toward destruction and unable to hit the brakes.

Then, one night, I ended up in a hot yoga class.

Spiritual Awakening

My friend Ashley invited me, and I went without thinking much about it. The studio smelled like lavender, with just enough Subway sandwich aroma drifting in from the shop next door. The heat pressed against my skin, thick and unrelenting, and within minutes, I was drenched. My leggings clung to me like a second skin. My muscles screamed in downward dog, a pose I used to do effortlessly in my gymnastics days. My arms trembled. I felt pathetic, but for the first time in a long time, I also felt alive.

Something shifted in me that night.

I signed up for the studio's two-week trial and started going every day. The weight started falling off, and though I still partied, it wasn't as frequent. Yoga felt like the answer I had been looking for. It was the first time I had ever slowed down, breathed deeply, and been present in my own body. The first time I had done something that wasn't for a man, a drink, or a fleeting high.

What I didn't realize at the time was that yoga isn't just stretching and breathing. It's rooted in ancient Eastern spiritual traditions designed to open the body and mind to altered states of consciousness. Many of the poses were originally offerings to Hindu deities, and the practice often encourages things like emptying the mind and connecting to a "higher self." At the time, none of that fazed me. I welcomed it all. It felt calming, grounding, even enlightening. And maybe our culture is so drawn to it because it feels good. It's great exercise. It soothes anxiety. It gives the sense that we're healing, growing, and getting more in tune with ourselves.

I didn't see anything wrong with it. I just knew I wanted more of whatever that feeling was. As I rolled up my yoga mat after class, a thought flickered in the back of my mind: *What if this was the answer? What if this was the thing that could fix me?*

I couldn't have known then that it was the beginning of something much bigger. It was the doorway into the next chapter of my life, one that would take me far from Michigan, deep into the world of New Age spirituality, and straight into the arms of people who would change my life forever.

I had no idea that the world I was stepping into would consume me, shape me, and ultimately, break me. And that one decision to follow the feeling of peace I found on that mat would lead me down a path I never could have imagined.

CHAPTER 4

LA GIRL: CHASING ILLUSIONS AND LOSING MYSELF

pril 2017. Just weeks before college graduation. I sat in the bar's lounge before my bartending shift, flipping through the book *You Are a Badass* by Jen Sincero. The principles Sincero presented convinced me that I wasn't just part of the universe but *I was* the universe itself, full of power, and it was time I started acting like it. Her teachings pushed the idea that our thoughts and beliefs shape our reality, that confidence and bold action could change our lives, and that we each carry the power to create our own destiny.

Oooh, I hold the power. The words ignited something in me, a mix of excitement and urgency. My pulse quickened. *I need to get it together and start making stuff happen. Yesterday.*

I had spent my entire life as an atheist, believing that science held all the answers, but now, for the first time, I was questioning everything. That book, that new way of thinking, was telling me that God wasn't a being but a force, an energy that flowed through everything. And if that was true, then I wasn't just a random person in the universe—I *was* the universe. I was the god of my own life. The realization felt both liberating and terrifying.

You know what? I need to follow the dreams of my heart. The universe has got my back. That kind of thinking wasn't just a quote on Pinterest anymore. It had become a way of life for me. I was reading all the right books: *The Universe Has Your Back, You Are a Badass, The Four Agreements,* and *The Power of Now.* They taught me that I could manifest my reality, raise my vibration, and trust my inner guidance above all else.

Without hesitation, I withdrew my plans to go to medical school and made a yoga Instagram to document my new journey. To my surprise, brands started reaching out, sending me yoga clothes, props, even skincare products in exchange for posts. Maybe it was a sign, I thought. Maybe the universe really was working in my favor.

Thoughts Like Clouds

I had officially discovered the world of self-help and mindfulness. It all promised that healing could only be found by going inward, never acknowledging God. That truth was relative, and power came from detaching from negativity. Eckhart Tolle taught me to "watch" my thoughts like clouds in the sky, as if freedom came from observation rather than transformation. It was appealing, even addictive, because it gave me the illusion of control. If I just stayed present enough, visualized hard enough, aligned with the right frequency, then everything I wanted would come to me. Success. Confidence. Peace. I didn't realize that this kind of faith in the universe was just a repackaged lie, one that's been recycled through the decades, from the '60s love-and-drugs movement to the spiritual influencers' era I was now participating in. It all promised light, and I clung to it.

But not everyone saw my new enlightenment that way. My hometown and college friends started pulling away, their judgments loud even when unspoken. Two friends even made a mocking Instagram account, exaggerating yoga poses and joking about how "he's found the light." At parties, people accused me of thinking I was better than them, and soon, I stopped going out as much. Their words shouldn't have mattered, but they did. Deep down, I still craved their approval.

My anxious thoughts were at war with my newfound sense of power. If I could just *heal myself* enough, I wouldn't care what anyone thought. I could manifest the life I wanted—fame, success, financial freedom. But the highs of these revelations never lasted. They were always followed by crashing lows, by moments of doubt and anxiety I couldn't shake. Still, I told myself it was just part of the process. *Growth isn't linear.*

Looking back, I see the void I desperately tried to fill, one that only Jesus could heal. But at the time, the Christian God felt restrictive, outdated. In the new spiritual world, everything was accepted. There was no single God, only energies and manifestations and the belief that your thoughts, energy, and intentions can shape your reality. Humans could manipulate the universe, bending it to their will. I was a slave to my ambition. It was never enough.

> My anxious thoughts were at war with my newfound sense of power. If I could just heal myself enough, I wouldn't care what anyone thought.

Manifestation is often paired with the law of attraction, which teaches that "like attracts like." So, if you think positively and believe hard enough, you'll attract good things. It's also tied to something called creative visualization, where you imagine the life you want in vivid detail—your dream house, relationship, career, or body—and trust that the "universe" will deliver it if you match the right frequency or mindset.

On the surface, it sounds empowering. Who wouldn't want to believe that they can shape their future simply by visualizing it or raising your vibration? It makes people feel like they're in control. That they're "co-creators with the universe." That they can manifest abundance, love, and success just by "aligning" with it. But here's the issue: It's a lie that places you at the center of your own universe.

New Age spirituality was intoxicating because it felt like love, but in reality, it was just self-worship. It gave me the illusion of control, convincing me I was my own god. Yet, was I truly feeling better? Maybe in flashes. But the deeper I went, the more exhausted I became. I held onto the belief of reincarnation, that after I die, my soul will be reborn into a new body. Maybe all the bad things I had experienced were just my karma working itself out, and I could earn my way into a better next life. For someone with bipolar II, the cycles of death and rebirth that New Age promoted—this constant need for self-transformation—was nothing short of dangerous. All of it was a hamster wheel that never stopped spinning.

But I wasn't ready to see that yet.

These beliefs are popular in Hinduism and Buddhism, and they are deeply embedded in New Age spirituality. And honestly, I can see why people gravitate toward them. They give an explanation for suffering ("it's your karma"), and they promise second chances through endless lives, as if you get unlimited do-overs until you finally get it right.

Yoga Teacher in Training

Determined to keep following my heart, I enrolled in a yoga teacher training course. I juggled bartending and social media while studying to get certified, convinced that sharing yoga was my purpose. When I was in a flow, moving through poses with music blasting in the background, I felt beautiful, powerful—almost untouchable. People may tell you that yoga is only a physical practice or philosophy, but in my training course, I was directly taught that it was a religion. It's often presented as a tool for flexibility, fitness, or stress relief, but its roots go much deeper. Yoga originated in ancient India as a spiritual discipline within Hinduism.

I had no idea the path I was stepping onto would lead me to some of the darkest places of my life.

Amy flipped her red hair extensions over her shoulder and smirked. "Amir told me I was the reason they won their football game," she proclaimed during yoga teacher training. She had been teaching "private yoga" to a few Detroit Lions players. With the body of a fitness model and an almost arrogant confidence, she was unapologetically bold, always boasting. *Is this girl actually for real?* I wondered. She was unlike anyone I had ever met, but over time, we started hanging out, going to the gym after training, and taking photos for our Instagrams. I was drawn to the confidence I initially found annoying. Unlike the self-deprecating, insecure people I was used to, Amy owned who she was. It was refreshing. She wanted to DO THINGS. Like I did.

Empowerment Becomes Exploitation

One day at the gym, Amy told me about an exciting new gig she had booked in Los Angeles.

"I'm going to be modeling in a production," she said. "It's in the mountains of Malibu, in a mansion, with other goddess yogis. We're getting paid $5,000 a day."

Malibu? Mansion? Money? Modeling? Mountains? My heart raced.

"Ummmm, where do I sign up?" I asked, practically salivating. I should mention it was a nude shoot. Should this have set off any red flags in my mind? Yes, but I was blinded by the glamour.

"I think all the spots are full," Amy said, "but maybe we can pull some strings."

A few weeks later, I was bartending my last shift during a home game for MSU. I was working the patio alone, which made it easy to embellish my tips. That day, I made the most money I'd ever made in a single shift. As I was counting my cash at closing, I got a text inviting me to the shoot.

The next day, I flew to Los Angeles without a second thought. Soon, I found myself in a Malibu mansion, getting my hair and makeup done, about to pose nude while doing yoga. My stomach twisted. *I can't turn back now.*

I walked downstairs, my hair and makeup perfect, only to see three models in three-legged dog, completely naked. A cold wave of realization hit me. *I didn't even have time to get a wax or a spray tan, for crying out loud.* But I was there. No backing out.

After the shoot, Amy and I returned home to Michigan and continued our yoga teacher training, but Amy had yet another proposition. She introduced me to an app called Seeking Arrangements. A platform where wealthy, mostly older men sought companionship, and women sought financial compensation.

After spending my college years hooking up with guys who were using me FOR FREE, I was very open to this business model. *I'm in control. I call the shots.*

I had no idea the damage it would do to my soul. I was just desperate to escape my home, to make money, to feel valuable.

With that, Amy and I packed up our things and set off on a cross-country road trip. Howard, the man who had arranged the yoga shoot, told us we had something "electric" between us—our dynamic, our look, our presence. He promised us success and a future in the nude yoga business.

I could tell you crazy stories about our detours during our drive: visiting friends in Nashville and Dallas, stopping to catch the sunrise at the Grand Canyon, spending a night in the penthouse of the Bellagio in Las Vegas with two Indian heirs (no, we didn't do anything with them; it's a long story), or getting a front-row table and free bottle service to see Nelly perform because a club promoter followed me on Instagram, the crazy drugs we tried. But I would be lying if I said those seemingly glamorous experiences weren't overshadowed by the worst anxiety I had ever felt in my life.

Looking back, I realize anxiety isn't always bad. It can be a warning sign, a way your soul cries out when you're walking into danger. I just didn't listen.

When we finally arrived in Los Angeles—with no home, no solid plan—Howard gave us the keys to a home in the Valley in Sherman Oaks. We found ourselves constantly running into celebrities, comedians, and producers. We kept meeting wealthy men through Seeking Arrangements. Was this really my dream? No. But I told myself it was a start. I believed if I just kept journaling, visualizing, and manifesting, the universe would hand me my dream life. I had to be patient and diligent.

Then something bad happened. Really bad.

My Darkest Decision

I was back in Michigan for a visit, working out at my hometown gym. Box jumps, handstands—my usual routine. Tiny sports bra, spandex shorts, Kendrick Lamar's "DNA" blasting in my ears. Clothes felt like a drag. Then I felt a tap on my shoulder.

I pulled out my headphones and turned around.

Mr. Nelson.

"Abby!? Is that you? I can't believe it's really you! Hi! Wow, you look great." His eyes flickered over me. "I heard you posted a video of yourself doing naked yoga. Is that true?"

My stomach tightened.

He was beaming. "That's just so cool," he continued. "I've been wanting to get into yoga. Bad knee, you know. Think you could help? Do you teach private lessons?"

I forced a polite smile, reassured him that yoga could definitely help, and left.

On my drive home, my phone lit up with a text.

Hi. It's Mr. Nelson. Come by my office on your way home. I have a business proposition for you.

I was surprised he even had my number.

I scoffed at his message. *Is he serious?* I could read between the lines. But somehow, my fingers opened my maps app and typed in his address.

When I stepped into his office, I sat stiffly in the chair across from his desk. Framed photos of his wife lined the walls along with Steph's senior pictures, my old "best friend," the girl who used to bully me. My stomach churned.

He leaned forward. "Would you do naked yoga for me?"

Something in me shut off. My mind blanked. A thick fog settled in my brain, dulling the edges of reality. The answer left my mouth before I could fully register it.

"Yes."

Make it stop.

His voice lowered. "Would you do something else for me right now?"

Pause. A heartbeat.

"Sure."

I watched as he closed the blinds.

I left his office with $1,000 in cash stuffed in my pocket.

I told myself it didn't matter. That it wasn't *real*. That I could compartmentalize, shove it into some locked box in my brain, and move forward like it never happened. Like *I* never happened. That was something I had learned to do well. I'd been slipping out of my own skin for years, drifting outside myself when life got too painful, too uncomfortable, too real. So, I dissociated. I buried it. And the affair began.

Mr. Nelson wasn't shy about taking me out to dinner, whispering secrets over candlelight like we were old confidants. I listened, detached, thinking how *stupid* he was. But the joke was on me, too.

"We have to take this to the grave," he warned one night. "If anyone finds out, both of our lives will be ruined."

I laughed, shaking my head. *Yeah, pretty sure YOUR life will be ruined. I think I'll be fine.*

I had no idea how wrong I was.

The affair continued. I lived in LA, but he would fly me back home whenever he wanted. And I let him.

Hollywood Dreams

In LA, Amy and I were still working with Howard on our naked yoga business, which mostly meant smoking joints with him on the rooftop of his Santa Monica office and showing him our choreographed routines. He was convinced that if we took these performances to strip clubs, we would become a sensation. "You'll make millions," he promised.

From the outside, it looked like I was on my way. I had a view of the marina, where seals would wake me each morning with their calls as golden sunlight streamed through my window. I had total freedom, spending my days at Muscle Beach with my yoga friends, filming content, attending high-end shoots, working out at the upscale sports club Equinox, and taking classes at the most exclusive yoga studios in LA.

But inside? I was empty.

The anxiety never left. The shame sat heavy on my chest, pressing down with every breath. And now, on top of it all, I had the judgment of others creeping in more than ever. Rumors about me were spreading. I had chased an illusion, and I was drowning in it.

I had surrounded myself with free-spirited people, raving about how we were all flowing with the universe, manifesting, and spreading love. I felt like I was part of a movement, connected to something bigger than myself. But at the end of each night, I was left alone with my tormenting thoughts.

I had believed that money and a glamorous lifestyle would fill the void inside me. That if I curated the perfect life, I would *become* the person I was pretending to be. But no matter how many high-end experiences I chased, how much attention I received, or how many luxury events I attended, it never filled the aching emptiness inside me. Instead of feeling empowered, I felt like a slave—to money, to status, to the image I had created.

The thing about illusions is that they always shatter.

I had spent so much time trying to make my external life look perfect, but the truth kept catching up with me. Sure, there were moments of glamour, but underneath it all, I wasn't nearly as successful or fulfilled as I wanted to be. I craved more. More validation, more followers, more of the life I saw in the influencers and celebrities I admired.

> I had believed that money and a glamorous lifestyle would fill the void inside me. That if I curated the perfect life, I would become the person I was pretending to be.

Deep down, I knew what I was living was only a cheap imitation of what I truly longed for. No amount of attention or approval could fill the ache inside me. Because what I was really searching for, what I had been desperate for all along, was something the world could never give me: real love, real purpose, real redemption. And that could only come from God.

But I wasn't ready to accept that yet.

My pride, my desires, my need for control kept me running. I still thought I could force my dream life into existence if I just tried harder, manifested more, meditated deeper, pushed past the anxiety. I refused to see that everything I was chasing was slipping through my fingers.

I spent hours visualizing my dreams in meditation, journaling about how I was going to change the world with love. And deep down, I *did* have good intentions, but they were tangled in lies, deception, greed, and lust. All things that God warns us against. I had unknowingly opened myself up to darkness, believing I was enlightened.

Looking back, I can see how my untreated bipolar II disorder played a role in it all. Grandiose dreams are common in manic states. I wasn't taking my meds because I was in denial that I had legitimate mental health issues. My unchecked emotions and ambitions pushed me deeper into deception, making it even harder to see the truth. My desperation to be part of something bigger only led me into more bondage, not freedom.

God was trying to pull me out. But I wasn't ready to listen. Not yet.

I would have to hit rock bottom—again and again—until I was finally willing to surrender. Until I was finally willing to let him save me.

I felt responsible for keeping Amy in check and managing our relationship with Howard, but she was entirely focused on partying and her social media. Through her, I met Wes, a club promoter who introduced me to new drugs I had never tried before, including ketamine.

The ketamine experience was intense and strangely spiritual. One night, crossing Hollywood Boulevard, I was so high that it felt like I had landed on another planet. I could barely make out the world around me. It was like walking through a twisted video game. These moments, while surreal, were also a wake-up call. Wes's life was consumed by drugs, and watching him spiral made me realize how easily addiction and escapism could take over. I later learned he had died, a sobering reminder of how dangerous that world could be.

Ketamine is everywhere in LA—clinics, prescriptions, street deals—but its popularity doesn't make it safe. The experience forced me to confront my choices and the path I was on, highlighting the emptiness and danger of searching for meaning in substances rather than in God, but not until much later. I was still drawn to experimenting with all sorts of drugs, thinking I was immune to their side effects. I now realize the spiritual dangers I was ignoring.

Damaged Goods

I was pushing my body to its limits. One day, I even pulled my hamstring while working out at Equinox, stretching in the outdoor turf area under the Santa Monica sun. My body felt unusually loose, like my legs were made of stretchy rubber bands. I flowed from left split to right split to middle, back and forth, enjoying the ease of movement. But as I slipped into one final right-leg split, something went wrong. The rubber band snapped. A sharp, sickening pain shot through my hamstring. *No. No, that didn't just happen.* I froze, refusing to accept it. *Maybe if I ignore it, it'll go away.* I was in denial until, finally, my entire right side became so swollen that

I couldn't walk. It was terrifying, especially considering my livelihood was largely dependent on my body and physical well-being. I spent three days at my apartment complex's pool, reading *A New Earth* by Eckhart Tolle with an icepack and ibuprofen. At the time, the book was the manuscript of my life perspective, a book I now recognize as full of insults and disrespect for God. It preached that salvation came through self-enlightenment, urging people to transcend their egos and awaken to a higher consciousness, essentially teaching that we could achieve peace and fulfillment without God. It was the same lie from the Garden of Eden: We could become like God on our own.

An older man from the East Coast named Ted approached me at the pool and asked what I was reading. He offered me a hit of weed. We ended up talking for hours as he inappropriately massaged my damaged hamstring, and a strange relationship started developing between us.

He told me all about his fall from success back in New York City. According to him, his ex-wife was a raging narcissist who turned his kids against him. He rolled with the big dogs in commercial real estate back in NYC, but he had stepped away from his volatile family situation, moved to California, and was waiting for the next big venture. He believed in the benefits of yoga and meditation I told him about. He told me that day that he and I were going to make something together. His confidence made me feel hopeful.

Meanwhile, Howard began singling me out more. He started inviting me to meetings and into his office, asking me to take notes and help him expand his marijuana businesses. I felt honored, like maybe I was on my way to becoming a real business professional.

One day, as I sat across from him in his office, he leaned forward and told me, "Whatever you dream of can come true. But if you don't visualize it the exact way, you'll end up getting the monkey's paw." I gazed into his eyes as he told me about the old tale of wishes granted but twisted, where people got what they asked for, only in the worst possible way. Just then, his face morphed into my father's. I blinked and shook my head, but I couldn't unsee it. It was as if my dad was sitting there, speaking those words to me.

Meanwhile, the "business" I thought I would co-own with him was nothing but a scam. Shocker. What I hadn't realized yet was that I was being groomed. Howard, the man who had promised me opportunity, sexually assaulted me. He thought he was being sly about it, calling me out of the blue one day and hyping up our business venture, then telling me how insecure I was. I thought it was a bit strange. He proceeded to ask me what I was getting him for Christmas and asked if I would meet him at his office to perform a dance for him. I hoped it wasn't what it sounded like. I went in there thinking I could do the dance and get out before anything happened. Lines were crossed, and I awkwardly put an end to it knowing that I would be punished for not giving him what he wanted. I know I'm writing this almost casually, but the truth is, it was devastating. Catastrophic things were happening back-to-back, and I barely had time to process one before the next hit. I knew my refusal to give him what he ultimately wanted would end badly, and so I walked away with whatever dignity I could salvage.

I felt like an outcast among Amy and our circle of free-spirited yogis. I was nursing a serious injury that would take years to heal. The dream of the naked yoga business—the one I had spent the last six months visualizing with obsessive hope—was crumbling. I didn't know how I'd provide for myself financially, and I had no idea where my life was headed. The judgment and gossip swirling around me only added to the pressure. It was all too much.

Ted gave me the confidence to walk away from Howard and Naked Yoga, but when I told him about the assault, it meant admitting the whole thing had been a scam. I was left with no paycheck, no plan, and no choice but to rely on an older man to take care of me—a man who was thirty years my senior, divorced, and (as I would soon learn) a mentally unstable drug addict.

Around this time, the affair with Mr. Nelson was becoming too much. I texted him and told him I wanted to stop.

Over the next few months, I fell into a deep depression. I had no one, so I spent my time with Ted. I distanced myself from Amy, who Ted described as "damaged goods," which he wasn't really wrong about. She had been taking advantage of me from the beginning, stealing my clothes and even calling me fat. She stayed involved with Howard. I couldn't help but blame her for introducing me to all of that mess. I'm just glad I never gave myself to Howard like she did.

Ted told me I couldn't go home in defeat, and I believed him. Together, we figured out a living situation that would work for both of us. We became roommates and moved into a small apartment in Playa Del Rey, a neighboring town. We had to have his brother cosign on our apartment because Ted was clearly struggling with finances, too. Not the most reliable option, but I was desperate.

It was obvious I was not in a good place, so he gave me muscle relaxers and magic mushrooms to help with my healing. I had taken them before, but this was the real start of my idolatry of mushrooms. Every month, almost like a ritual, Ted and I would trip on mushrooms together. Mushrooms had a powerful effect that I couldn't deny. In the context of the New Age, mushrooms are perceived as tools for consciousness expansion, personal growth, and spiritual exploration. I believed the mushrooms were healing me and revealing things to me. That the crying, snotting, shaking, and emotional breakdowns were trauma releasing from my body. I told myself that I was facing my pain in order to build myself back up. I thought I was being brave. I thought I was evolving. I truly believed all of this was necessary and needed to happen for me to move forward in life and be the person I was meant to be.

Although I placed my faith in the wrong person, Ted stayed true to his word, and we started our own business together—Abbyville.

CHAPTER 5

THE ABBYVILLE DREAM: WELLNESS, HEARTBREAK, AND DECEPTION

"**Y**ou can't go home with yuh tail between yuh legs," Ted reasoned, in his thick New York accent.

Eyes wide, I nodded slowly in agreement. *He's right*, I thought. *It's time for me to show my family and my haters who's boss.*

"I wasn't lyin' when I said we'd start something together," he said. "I've been workin' on this concept . . . we'll call it Abbyville."

Oooh, did I hear my name?

He came close, put his left arm around me, and motioned his right hand toward imaginary stars as he spoke. "Abbyville: The Wellness Concierge for the Mind Body and Soul. It's gonna be huge."

I smiled. "Hmm, a little wordy, but I can get down with it."

"We'll market it to seniors. Assisted living is a multimillion-dollar industry. We'll start there. Teach yoga and wellness programs to old people."

I got to work making flyers and posted them at local coffee shops. I went cold-knocking at assisted living homes to sell the programs that I hadn't even developed yet. Mind you, I had never done sales in my life and am a highly anxious person. Talk about smoke and mirrors.

One thing led to another, and before I knew it, I was leading a Holocaust survivor in a meditation, doing arts and crafts projects with stroke survivors, and teaching yoga to a woman who danced with Judy Garland back in the day. I taught laughter yoga, organized music video workshops, and even hosted a senior fashion show. I spent two months in a memory care intensive unit leading crafts and yoga for people who didn't know where they were. It was something special.

One day, I came home to a notice from the leasing office on our apartment door. It was a letter warning us to stop throwing cigarette butts off our balcony. Ted had told me that he quit smoking two years before and proclaimed his innocence. But I started seeing them for myself right under our balcony, and a few days later, I caught him in the act. The lies started unfolding. From finding out he lied to me about his age to learning he was a full-blown drug addict. On frequent occasions, we would take muscle relaxers together, and we smoked weed almost every day, but I didn't know he was on the muscle relaxers 24/7. Suddenly I realized our business was going to sink fast if he kept it up. He had originally told me he was forty-seven, but all it took was a quick glance at his driver's license to find out he was actually fifty-six. I wondered if anything he told me true.

Meanwhile, my lack of boundaries surfaced in full force with him. Although sleeping together wasn't part of our arrangement, he gave me massages, and we definitely had more than a professional relationship. He insisted that he was helping me recover from my injury, and he reassured me he didn't see us as a couple, but finding out all of his lies shook me into reality a bit. It was really creepy. *What am I doing?* I told him I was going to start dating other people, and he lost his mind. He wanted complete control over me.

Things escalated to a terrifying level. One night, Ted threatened to release photos of me, pictures he had taken without my consent. He was always taking pictures of me. Panic surged through me as I grabbed his phone, desperate to delete them. He tackled me, trying to wrestle it back. We fought, grappling onto the back balcony. It was insane, one of the craziest moments of my life. Somehow, I managed to push him off me and delete the photos, but the reality of my situation was undeniable. It was really dangerous. The guy was insane. I had to get out.

Also, despite my hard work on the business, we struggled to pay the bills. I was traveling all over Los Angeles to find more clients. I was no longer on Seeking Arrangements, but the shame of my past haunted me. I had daily nightmares. Memories of old friends and burned bridges consumed me. I couldn't even look people in the eyes when I was out in public. I was empty, lost, and mentally unraveling. Looking back, I can confidently say my demons had taken over.

Financial instability even affected my ability to afford food. I had lost so much weight, I was down to 110 pounds, my ribs visible beneath my skin. As if things weren't bad enough, I let Ted borrow my car one day. He was on muscle relaxers and nearly crashed, and he later scratched up my car trying to pull out of our parking garage. When I confronted him, he lashed out, screaming that I grew up in a barn and that my parents

> I couldn't even look people in the eyes when I was out in public. I was empty, lost, and mentally unraveling.

had "done a number on me." His manipulation was relentless. The walls were closing in. My life didn't even feel like it was mine anymore.

Then I met Cody.

Between Two Men and a Breaking Point

The dating app Hinge "highly suggested" Cody and I meet. He lived in Hermosa Beach. We met up at a bar in Manhattan Beach. His eyes sparkled as we bonded over our love for the band Rainbow Kitten Surprise. We had matching armband tattoos. Our parents were divorced, and our fathers were both wrestlers who had their ups and downs. He felt familiar. It didn't hurt either that I was hanging out with someone my age for the first time in eight months. I could feel my real self coming back to life with each sip of wine.

But the red flags were there, even from the beginning. During our first date, as we talked about music, he casually mentioned his friend Karissa, a girl he played music with. I didn't think much of it at first, but as we dated, something about their friendship started to feel off. She had a boyfriend, yet it was as if she wanted ownership over Cody, like she needed to be his number one. When he told me she had once tried to drunkenly kiss him, I brushed it off, but my unease only grew. Before long, I started battling paranoia, convinced something was happening between them behind my back. I had never felt that kind of fear or anxiety in a relationship before, and it was almost debilitating.

One night, he invited me out with his friends. I got drunk with them, laughing, feeling alive, but woke up with the worst hangover since high school.

Meanwhile, Ted warned me against Cody. He predicted that

this group of people was bad for me, that Cody was just a boy, and I needed a man.

Things grew dangerous between Ted and me as I spent more time I spent with Cody. I knew I had to leave. The pandemic gave me the perfect excuse. I told everyone I had lost my clients due to COVID-19. In truth, my business had failed.

I texted Cody that I was leaving town for family reasons. I was too embarrassed to explain the real state of my life. Little did I know I was nearing Jesus, but this was not my last rock bottom. Life would darken once more before I found the light.

I left without telling Ted, my roommate and business partner, and headed home to Michigan. He always told me I needed professional help, so when he asked where I had gone, I simply replied, "I'm going to get the help I need."

New Job, Old Wounds

My dad flew out to LA to drive with me back home. I knew so much had changed. I had made a mess of my life in a desperate attempt to leave the chaos and strife at my childhood home in Michigan, and now I was headed back there. And going home wasn't easy. My siblings weren't exactly thrilled to see me. I think part of it was embarrassment. Word had spread around our small town about the choices I'd made, including posing naked on camera, and having *that* sister wasn't something they were proud of. But I sensed something else beneath the surface, maybe even resentment. I had escaped. I'd gone off to California to live however I wanted while they stayed behind in the thick of our family's dysfunction. I was supposed to be the big sister, but instead I had nearly abandoned them. I failed in ways I wish I hadn't. I hope they understand that, at the time, I left because I didn't know how else to survive.

I immediately pursued a career in pharmaceutical sales. I reasoned that if I could build a business from the ground up, then working for a corporation with endless resources would be easy. And I was right.

Pharmaceutical sales carried a certain prestige: fancy cars, business trips, and a solid paycheck. After several failed ventures, I felt like I couldn't show up in the world without something impressive attached to my name. While many were losing jobs during the pandemic, I landed one. A major pharmaceutical company offered me a position and relocated me to Cincinnati. For the first time, I had my own apartment that truly felt like mine. I decorated it with an eclectic mix of styles and paid for everything myself.

Feeling accomplished with my new job, car, apartment, and salary, I reached back out to Cody. He was so happy for me and my new life in Cincinnati.

A few months later, my college girlfriends and I took a trip down the California coast. I told Cody I'd be in LA, and we planned to meet. I promised myself I wouldn't sleep with him. My chest tingled as I stuck my head out of the sunroof riding down the Pacific Coast Highway. We were getting closer to LA. Cody and I planned to meet at a rooftop bar in Venice. I saw him on the other end of the crosswalk. We walked toward each other, and a smile came over my face.

We had a magical time together that night, and in the end, he convinced me to sleep with him. He said he wanted to connect with me in that way, and I didn't know how to say no. I hated how easy it was for him to break my boundaries, how effortlessly I let it happen. It was a familiar feeling, one I had ignored too many times before. I should have seen the cause for concern in his behavior.

But I was drawn to him, to his adventurous spirit, our shared love for music, our bond from having complicated fathers. The next morning, we covered Rainbow Kitten Surprise's "First Class." He played guitar while I sang. I was head over heels.

Before I had even left LA to go back to Cincinnati, all I could think about was when we could see each other again. A few weeks later, he visited me. I felt like I was in a dream. We floated down the Miami River, listened to James Blake, and sang Kid Cudi songs in my apartment. We got tattoos. Mine was a butterfly with magic mushrooms as one of the wings; his was an astronaut. I told him we should date. He said long-distance wasn't healthy for him. I should have believed him.

I didn't.

Next, I flew to LA, hoping he'd change his mind. We went to Mammoth, a lake town in California's Sierra Nevada, for his friend's birthday. While tripping on mushrooms, we stared at the stars, and he told me he'd regret it forever if he lost me.

He asked me to be his girlfriend. I accepted.

We traveled back and forth across the country. High highs, low lows. We took road trips all over California, from wandering through Joshua Tree and ski towns, to San Bernardino, camping under the stars, swimming in hot springs, and being blown away by the wild beauty of nature. Those moments only deepened my feelings for him. Eventually, I moved in with him and found a new pharmaceutical sales job on the West Coast. But something was off with his friend group, especially his friendships with other girls. I noticed how they acted when I was around. They were quiet, exchanging glances, like I was an outsider in my own relationship.

Meanwhile, I was going through a weird phase myself. My passion for music burned stronger than ever. I dreamed of writing an album and becoming famous. Cody had a talent for music production. I fantasized about us becoming artists together. I was the only one who had that dream, though.

I spiraled deeper into the New Age. I bought my first tarot deck. One night, I lit candles, wrote my intentions, and did my first reading with the Green Witch deck. The cards told me that despite financial security, I felt insecure. The statement applies to everyone to some extent, but in that moment, I believed I had a powerful gift.

I declared myself a Green Witch. I picked up a book called *Witch: Unleashed. Untamed. Unapologetic* by Lisa Lister, who is widely known in New Age and modern spiritual feminism. Her mission is to reclaim the word "witch" as sacred, intuitive, and healing, not evil. She argues that the term has been demonized by a patriarchal system trying to silence powerful women. I was hooked. I began to believe that witchcraft held the key to who I truly was.

I dressed like one. Got more tattoos. Micro-dosed mushrooms and weed, even at work. My ego inflated. I pierced my nose, chopped my hair, dyed it different colors, and got bangs. I randomly came out as bisexual on my social media. I even came out as transgender. It was popular at the time for people to update their pronouns, and I changed mine to "they/them." Not because I truly was, but because I had been so hurt as a woman, I didn't want to be one anymore.

All the while I was dealing with immense guilt about the affair with Mr. Nelson. It was coming up in my dreams. It was the first thing I thought about in the morning and the last thing I thought about at night. I finally made the decision to tell his kids because the guilt was eating me alive. I figured they deserved to know the truth. If I were in their shoes, I would want someone to tell me, so that is what I did. They asked all the right questions, and I know they knew I was telling the truth. Even so, they decided to deny it and block me on social media. I felt better getting it off my chest, but it still didn't sit right with me. He was getting away with it, and I looked like the only bad guy. I could feel in my gut that rumors were spreading, and I couldn't bear it. I wished someone would confront me instead of me feeling their judgments from afar.

Meanwhile Cody seemed apathetic to finding out about my past, my sexual identity labels, and my beliefs about witchcraft and New Age. Deep down, I think he was hurt that I had ghosted him before. We both had trust issues.

The truth was, despite my issues and messy past, I was devoted to him. In my heart, I wanted marriage and kids, but he wanted to keep me at arm's length.

He always told me what I wanted to hear. Even after I got fired from my job while trying to relocate to LA and taking a new pharmaceutical sales job in Hermosa Beach, things got so bad between us. I continued to collect crystals, meditate, journal, and try to manifest. I still had my dreams of being rich and famous, but this time, I wanted to be a famous artist, like Billie Eilish. I started exploring singing and writing.

All I wanted when I was with Cody was to be able to break out in the songs that were rushing through my head at all times. But around him, I couldn't muster a sound. At the time, I thought my throat chakra must have been blocked—my fault again. I wondered if I could ever heal myself enough to let out the voice I knew was inside.

There were certain times under the influence of alcohol that I let my voice out loudly, but Cody never validated it. Sometimes on mushrooms I would let my voice out, and it felt so freeing. But when the intoxication wore off, it was gone.

Birth Chart Obsessed

I also loved updating my Instagram followers that I was a double Capricorn and shared pictures of the full moon. Astrology was honestly my biggest obsession out of all the New Age practices.

I was completely hooked. What started off as harmless curiosity—asking people "What's your sign?"—quickly spiraled into a full-blown identity study. I knew I was a *Capricorn sun*, and I later learned I was also a *Capricorn rising*. That combination meant I was supposed to be smart, ambitious, and successful, a go-getter with discipline, loyalty, and honesty. Basically, the know-it-all who gets things done. It felt like a power combo. But at the same time, I never quite felt as overly serious as Capricorns were described to be. So, imagine how validated I felt when I discovered I was born on the *cusp of Sagittarius.*

The cusp of *prophecy,* they called it. Wild, right? Just the name alone made me feel special. Sagittariuses were known to be adventurous, creative, magnetic, and free-spirited. Combine that with my Capricorn side and boom. Apparently, I had the "best of both worlds" to make all my dreams come true. Talk about a dangerous mindset for someone already struggling with bipolar disorder. I felt so strongly about my purpose and identity in astrology that I even have the word "Prophecy" tattooed permanently on my hand, with the earth sign symbol on my finger.

PROPHECY

My "Prophecy" tattoo serves as a reminder that
deception once made me feel chosen by the universe,
before I knew I was already chosen by God.

It didn't stop there. I went on to learn that my *moon was in Virgo*, which meant I was analytical, detail-oriented, and emotionally reserved, and my *Venus was in Scorpio*, meaning I supposedly loved with depth, mystery, and intensity. I had a blend of earth and water signs, and I devoured every little description like it was a divine message. I read horoscopes religiously, checked moon phases daily, and broke down my friends' and exes' birth charts like a detective solving cosmic puzzles. It wasn't just a hobby; it became a full-time lens through which I saw myself and the world. A false sense of self built on the stars.

It was honestly just self-obsession in disguise. Astrology made me feel seen, understood, and validated. It gave me something to *belong* to, something to explain the chaos in my life. But the deeper I went, the more I realized how much of a distraction it really was. It hooks you in with just enough truth to keep you coming back for more. There are seeds of truth, of course. That's what makes it so convincing. But it never ends. There's always a new retrograde, a new moon, a new placement. It's a hamster wheel of "discovery" that only pulls you further away from truth and deeper into deception.

While I was obsessing over the stars, Cody was constantly taking the side of his friends, who didn't like me. I think they thought I was stealing Cody away from them. I would find myself crying in the bathroom on a regular basis. My anxiety before was nothing compared to the anxiety I felt in this toxic relationship.

The Truth About Sexual Liberation

At that time, I believed that my body was my power. I used it to get what I wanted, to feel in control, to manipulate, to survive. The world told me that it was freedom, that it was empowerment,

The lie of sexual liberation had me in chains, and I didn't even see it.

but in reality, it was a slow erosion of my self-worth. I could act as though I was untouchable, but inside, I was breaking. The lie of sexual liberation had me in chains, and I didn't even see it.

The New Age concept of sacred sexuality taught me that sex can be sacred, holy, and that connecting with your "twin flame" through sexual union is a spiritual experience that aligns you with the universe. Though it is framed as a way of becoming more attuned to your higher self, it is a distortion of God's design for sex and marriage.

The idea of twin flames in New Age teachings is one of the most dangerously misleading beliefs I encountered. A twin flame is often described as your "other half," someone whom you're spiritually meant to be with. Your soulmate, but on a deeper level. The idea is that twin flames are two halves of the same soul that were separated and now must reunite. This sounds beautiful and romantic, and I believed it fully when I met Cody. I was convinced that he was my twin flame, my perfect match, and the universe had brought us together.

I remember one moment in particular that should have felt like love but instead made me feel hollow. Cody and I had been together for a while. He was the first man I believed I could see a future with, the one I told myself would be different. If I gave him all of me, if I was everything he needed, he would stay, and we would build a life together. That's what I thought.

But the moment our intimacy ended, reality hit like a wave crashing into a fragile sandcastle. The warmth of his touch was gone, replaced by the cold silence of the room. He turned away, reaching for his phone, scrolling mindlessly, while I lay beside him, staring at the ceiling, feeling everything I had just given to him slip away. I swallowed the lump in my throat, trying to convince myself that I wasn't feeling what I knew deep down: It wasn't love.

"Are you okay?" I finally asked, hoping for reassurance, hoping he would pull me in and make me feel like I hadn't made another mistake.

"Yeah, I'm fine," he said, barely looking up. No warmth, no depth, no sign that what had just happened meant anything to him.

And suddenly, I couldn't hold it in anymore. The tears came, uninvited and uncontrollable. I turned away, trying to stifle them, not wanting to seem weak, but I felt my chest tighten, my stomach twist. I had done everything the world told me I should do to be loved, yet I felt more alone than ever.

He sighed. "Why are you crying?"

"I don't know," I whispered. I did know, but I didn't have the words for it yet. I felt empty, used. I had given him my body, hoping it would translate into love, but all it had done was leave me feeling unseen, misunderstood, and disposable.

I wanted to believe sex was just an expression of love, that it was just a natural part of a relationship. But deep down, something was telling me that it wasn't supposed to feel like this. It wasn't supposed to make me question my worth. It wasn't supposed to leave me feeling like I had poured out everything I had, only to be met with indifference.

What I didn't realize at the time was that this belief was leading me to place my value and identity in a relationship rather than in Christ. The truth is, not every person we connect with is meant to be a romantic partner, let alone a soulmate. In my obsession with this idea of a twin flame, I ignored the deeper spiritual implications of what was really happening. I made choices based on a New Age belief that pushed me further away from God's plan for relationships and marriage.

That was the deception of sexual freedom. The world told me that withholding sex was prudish, that waiting until marriage was outdated, that a woman should own her sexuality. But what they didn't tell me was the cost. The way it eats away at your soul. The way it ties you to people who have no intention of staying. The way it conditions you to settle for momentary pleasure instead of lasting commitment.

And yet, it wasn't until I met Jesus that I understood the full weight of what I was doing to myself. He didn't tell me sex was bad. He told me it was sacred. He didn't shame me for my past. He called me into something better. He showed me that sex was never meant to be casual, that it was meant to be a bond within a covenant, a reflection of something holy, not something thrown away.

When I finally chose purity, it wasn't because I became righteous overnight. It was because I was exhausted from giving away pieces of myself and getting nothing in return. I wanted real love, a love that mirrored God's design, one that wasn't conditional on how much I could offer physically. And that decision, that surrender, was what led me to true freedom.

CHAPTER 6

FULL-ON CRASH OUT

At a party in Hermosa Beach, I felt watched and unwelcome. The house music grated on me, and the energy in the room was tense. "Are you ready to leave?" I whispered to Cody. He was too worried about his friends' opinions to say yes. Instead, he stalled like he always did, either making us sneak out or asking permission to go.

I had shared one of my favorite artists, Sebastian Paul, with his friends earlier that night. They liked the music, but the vibe was still off. Eventually, I walked out on my own and waited in the driveway, exhausted from pretending. As I walked out, they blasted "On Some High"—the exact song I'd shown them—almost like they were mocking me. *Could that really be happening?*

A stranger who left the party at the same time asked if I was okay. When I said I had a boyfriend and pointed to Cody still inside, the man just shook his head. "Where is he?" he asked. I didn't know how to explain it, but somehow he seemed to understand what I was too blind to admit: Cody wasn't standing up for me. Not that night, not ever.

When Cody finally came out, he rambled about how happy he was and that he wanted to marry me. That kind of talk kept me hooked. We went home, listened to Lana Del Rey, and he passed out in his chair before collapsing onto the floor. The next day, when I brought it up, he denied the fall entirely, as if it never happened. I started wondering if I was going crazy.

A few days later, I vividly remember having a conversation with my nana, who is a Christian. I explained to her that we both believe in the same God, but I don't call mine a father, and I don't put labels on him. She told me we certainly did not believe in the same God because she believes in God the Father. Her words stuck with me: "If you don't know who you are praying to, you can be susceptible to evil." That night, a seed was planted. Her prayers for me would continue, waiting to be answered.

I finally told Cody one day that I thought we should take a break from having sex because I would cry and feel drained of all my power and energy every time. He was sucking the life out of me.

Cody declined. Everything came to a head. I couldn't take it anymore, being humiliated by his lack of loyalty to me and him always choosing his friends over me. The constant tears and paranoia that he was cheating on me. I was devastated. We broke up, and I moved out of our studio apartment in Hermosa Beach and into an even smaller studio apartment in Westchester. I went full-on manic, having the worst outbreak of my life. I blasted him and others on my social media page and started bringing my wellness and yoga practices to clients in my corporate pharmaceutical job, which was clearly a conflict of interest.

One evening, I needed to get to a work party at a client's office. I brought along my friend Ashley, the one who introduced me to yoga originally. I was trying to get her a job at the pharmaceutical company I worked for. The neighboring office was run by an older man who was a small-business owner. I'll call him Joe. We got to talking, and I told him about my love for yoga. He said he had been wanting to get into it. We exchanged contact information, but then I forgot about the conversation.

Ashley listened as I vented about my broken heart over Cody, and she recommended I begin seeing a psychic. She said that it may offer healing and clarity. So, I made an appointment and began seeing the Hermosa Beach psychic, who clearly picked up that I was having a mental breakdown. She told me I was deeply wounded and weak and that she wanted to help me.

The Worst Spiritual Trap

The room smelled like incense and something faintly metallic, like coins rubbed between fingertips. Dim candlelight flickered against the walls, casting strange shadows on the collection of trinkets surrounding me. Crystals, religious idols, tarot decks, and charms cluttered the wooden shelves, each one promising enlightenment, healing, or protection.

I sat across from the psychic, my heart pounding as I poured out my troubles, desperate for answers. My words spilled out like vomit, every thought, doubt, and frustration rolling off my lips and into her ears.

She sucked me in by telling me things other people wouldn't know, but then she told me that I had been introduced to an older man who would become a source of love and abundance for me. At first, I truly didn't know what she was talking about, but then I realized, low and behold, I was in contact with Joe and had started giving him yoga lessons, about to fall back into an old habit I thought I had kicked.

She nodded solemnly, as if she had already seen it all coming. Her gaze flickered toward a towering crystal that gleamed under the candlelight. It stood nearly two feet tall, deep violet with veins of gold twisting through it. I hadn't noticed it before, but now it was all I could see.

"This," she whispered, her voice laced with mystery, "is what you need."

A slight gust of wind brushed against my skin, though no windows were open.

"This crystal has powerful healing properties," she continued. "It will remove all the impurities inside of you. Everything you desire—peace, love, clarity—it will bring to you. But you must act fast. It was meant for you."

Her words slithered into my ears, convincing and sweet like honey. It was as if she had taken a master-level sales course on spiritual desperation. Then she dropped the price: $6,000.

I hesitated. It was an absurd amount of money. But the crystal wouldn't leave my mind. It was like it had hooked itself into me, whispering that I needed it. It was calling me.

Days passed, and I still couldn't shake the pull. I felt like I was losing my grip on reality. I had to have it.

Like Gollum with the One Ring in *The Lord of the Rings*, I obsessed. *My precious.*

So, I sent the first payment. And the moment I did, a rush of energy flooded through me, like I had just unlocked some hidden power.

That night, I placed the crystal on my chest as I lay in bed, believing it was soaking up all my pain, all my brokenness. Whenever I felt low, I'd text the psychic, and she'd send me more "energy." I had no idea how it worked, only that it felt real.

Until it started to feel *too* real.

One night, I woke up frozen. Sleep paralysis. I couldn't move, couldn't scream. I looked toward the window and saw what I thought was a shadowy figure lurking there. The psychic.

Though imaginary, the figure seemed so real as it sat on the edge of my bed and silently watched me. And in that moment, I knew I had given her permission to enter my life in ways I didn't understand.

When you come into agreement with the New Age, when you give it permission, it will take hold of you. Tarot was dangerous enough, but psychics are a thousand times worse. They set spiritual traps for the vulnerable and the desperate, and I was both.

The psychic I saw didn't just give me "guidance." She drained my bank account and left me spiritually exposed. I handed over thousands of dollars, but worse, I unknowingly gave demons access into my life. My mental and emotional health unraveled after that. To this day, I can't believe how tightly I was held captive by the dark spirits I had invited in. The only reason I am free now is because in Christ, those spirits no longer have permission or authority over me.

Around the same time, my job discovered I had been bringing my essential oils into doctors' offices, and they fired me. My world spiraled again, worsened by my unchecked bipolar II disorder and my New Age practices. I was pulling tarot cards almost every day, frantically trying to gain control of my life.

I confided in Joe, and what began under the guise of helping him with his businesses quickly turned into something else. He took me on a vacation to Mexico. I convinced myself I wasn't slipping back into old destructive patterns, but I was. Once again, I found myself depending on an older man, this time thirty-four years my senior. He became my whole world. I had no other friends.

Meanwhile, I was haunted—by the psychic, by shadowy experiences, and by flashbacks of childhood trauma that surfaced with new intensity. I made accusations. I poured my pain out publicly on social media. I felt like my world was crumbling. And the psychic? She only confirmed my fears, encouraging me to keep pursuing Joe. She knew the longer I stayed entangled with him, the longer I would stay entangled with her. The more she drained me, the more she profited. I remained in bondage to her for eight long months.

CHAPTER 7

ROCK-BOTTOM REDEMPTION

Another day in my self-made prison. I sat in Joe's house, staring at the golden light spilling over Hermosa Beach, aching to be outside, to feel free. But the thought of being seen with him made my stomach twist. The shame of being seen next to a man old enough to be my father was unbearable. Every time he opened his mouth, another wave of embarrassment crashed over me. And yet, I had chosen that life. Hadn't I?

More like stumbled into it and clung on for dear life after losing my job in a manic spiral. An outburst of unresolved anger, heartbreak, and pride had cost me everything. But going home to Michigan? That wasn't an option. I would rather be anywhere else, with anyone else, than face the wreckage waiting for me there.

I forced myself to agree to a walk with Joe, cringing as he laced his fingers through mine. Every step felt like I was dragging a weight behind me. I kept my head down, dodging eye contact, praying no one saw me. But Joe? He was performing, as always. Name-dropping. Boasting. Talking about the time he crossed paths with Lady Gaga's creative director, the big Hollywood role he almost landed. It was exhausting, the way he clung to fading glimmers of a life he never truly had.

I wanted to disappear.

But I couldn't. Because I was stuck.

Joe was my financial stability, and I had willingly put myself in this cage. I told myself it was temporary. That this was just part of the process. After all, I was chasing my dreams, taking commercial acting classes, getting professional headshots, pouring money into piano and singing lessons. Surely, this was the sacrifice it took to finally make it. At least, that's what my psychic had told me. "Keep going," she said. "You're so close."

But I was unraveling. There was constant turmoil between Joe and me—arguments, tension, the suffocating weight of unspoken truths. I had never been more stressed in my life. And that was saying a lot.

Our entire dynamic was warped. He was clinging desperately to his youth. Struggling with addiction. Trapped in his own delusions. And me? I was convincing myself I could fix things, ignoring the screaming red flags. We had an unspoken deal: He provided security, and in return, I gave him my body. Not love. Not desire. Just obligation. Not even my past relationships with Ted or Howard involved this kind of obligation. I told myself it wasn't what it was. That I was in control. But my body knew the truth.

There were nights I would break down completely, sobbing so hard it felt like my soul was trying to claw its way out. Joe would ask if I was okay, and I would lie. "Oh, yeah. It's just a release." As if it was normal. As if I wasn't crumbling inside.

One time when Joe and I took mushrooms, he spent his trip in his bedroom crying. He was dealing with a mess of a life he made too. I left him alone and drew in my sketchbook, journaled, and sang as I did it. I let my voice out so loudly, I felt on top of the world. When I went to check on him, he cried and told me my voice sounded beautiful. That kind of validation was all I needed. Someone that heard me.

The next day when we reflected on what had happened the previous night, he told me he could hear me "humming quietly" and invalidated my voice. Except this time, I could pick up on the manipulation.

Then there was Joe's daughter. She was just a few years younger than me. And despite everything I was tangled up in, she carried something I didn't understand, a quiet confidence, a peace that I had never known. She was a Christian.

The irony would almost be laughable if it weren't so sad. There I was, drowning in darkness, yet launching a YouTube channel about manifestation, preaching to others about creating their dream life, about aligning with the universe. I was determined to convince people I had it all figured out. That I was winning. Deep down, I knew it was a lie. But hey, that's what all the self-help gurus said, right? Fake it until you make it. Thanks a lot, Jen Sincero.

Then came Father's Day in June of 2022. We all went out to eat, and Joe's daughter wearily asked me about my channel. I went into my well-rehearsed spiel, excited to share my wisdom. But she wasn't impressed. Instead, she tilted her head and said, "I don't believe in that. I know that any blessing that comes into my life is from God, not because I manifested it. I trust him to do his will in my life."

Her words hit me like a gut punch. No one had ever confronted me like that before.

I scrambled for a response. "What? I believe in God, too. I believe that, too." But the truth was, I didn't even know what I believed anymore. Her words haunted me long after that dinner.

The Moment I Was Set Free

The next morning, Joe and I went through our usual routine of meditation. By then, I was desperate. Empty. Exhausted. I had spent years chasing meaning, clawing for success, running from my past. But I had run out of places to hide.

So, I prayed.

Not to the universe. Not to my spirit guides. Not to whatever New Age deity I had put my faith in that week. Just to someone. To whoever was listening.

I prayed for truth. For peace. For something real. For an end to the pain. For healing.

And then, in the silence, something shifted. I didn't hear a voice or see a vision. But deep in my soul, I knew. It was like Saul on the road to Damascus, a man who was once blind to the truth, even persecuting believers, until he suddenly saw everything with piercing clarity after encountering Jesus. At the time of my salvation, I didn't even know who Saul was. But later, when I read the Bible for the first time on my own, his story struck me deeply. I opened my eyes, and I was not the same.

I didn't question it. I didn't fight it. I simply obeyed. From that moment on, I never gave my body away again. I walked away from everything that had enslaved me, rebuking the psychic once and for all. And for the first time in my life, I was free. I had spent years searching for truth. Truth had finally found me.

I remember the exact moment I realized that Jesus was the truth. The scales fell off my eyes, just like the saying claims. In an instant, I could finally see things clearly. It was as if my entire life, I had been walking in darkness without realizing it, and suddenly, the light turned on. As the classic hymn says: "I once was lost, but now am found; was blind, but now I see." I had spent years searching for comfort, fulfillment, joy, and peace, but for the first time, at age twenty-seven, I actually *felt* it. A peace so deep, so real, that it nearly took my breath away. Even though my life was still in turmoil and I had no idea what my future would look like, I felt a peace I didn't know existed, like I had stopped struggling and, for the first time, was being *held*. I felt *safe*.

It's hard to even describe the weight of what I'm saying, but when you have been searching for something your entire life and then, in a single moment, you *find it*—or rather, *he finds you*—it changes everything. That peace didn't come from within me. It wasn't something I achieved through meditation, affirmations, or mindset shifts. It wasn't temporary or circumstantial. It wasn't even something I felt like I chose. It just happened. It was Jesus. "Come to me, all of you who are weary and carry heavy burdens, and I will give you rest" (Matthew 11:28 NLT).

PART 2
FOUND IN CHRIST

CHAPTER 8

THE PRAYER THAT CHANGED EVERYTHING

My first encounter with Jesus wasn't what you might expect. Was it radical? Yes. Will I remember it for the rest of my life? Absolutely.

I didn't hear an audible voice, nor did I see him face to face. Instead, I felt something stir deep within me. It was a movement in my spirit so strong that I knew it wasn't my own thoughts. While there were no words, the message was crystal clear: "Stop having sex before marriage."

That was it. A single directive that would change the trajectory of my life in ways I couldn't yet comprehend.

I was meditating next to Joe when the revelation hit me. Without hesitation, I turned to him and told him what had just happened. As you can probably guess, he wasn't thrilled. But what could he say? This time, I had Jesus on my side. And from that moment forward, he would never leave me.

Certain in the Uncertain

I returned to my tiny 500-square-foot studio apartment in Westchester, but nothing felt the same. The walls of deception that had upheld my life for twenty-seven years were crumbling before my eyes. I stood there, watching them burn, in complete awe of what was happening. I didn't even fully understand who Jesus was yet, but I knew this: He was my savior, and I was about to learn the magnitude of what he had done for me.

But before that could happen, I had to unlearn the lies I had built my life upon. I didn't know what was next, but I felt an overwhelming peace. Relief washed over me, even as uncertainty loomed. I had no idea how I would navigate my way out of the relationship, the lifestyle, the identity I had carefully crafted. So, I did the only thing I could do—I prayed.

I didn't even fully understand who Jesus was yet, but I knew this: He was my savior, and I was about to learn the magnitude of what he had done for me.

For the first time, I prayed to my heavenly Father instead of to an ambiguous god. I am a lifelong journaler, so I used my journal to talk to God. I asked him specific questions and asked for specific answers because life had never been so uncertain and certain at the same time.

How was I going to get out of my Los Angeles apartment lease? I had no income besides my monthly checks from Joe. Those would surely stop as the nature of our arrangement was clearly going to change. Where would I go? I couldn't return to Michigan to a chaotic and explosive environment that had hurt me for years. How was I going to tell Joe that I had not been honest about my intentions and feelings for him? It was a mess.

A Family Rejoices

One of the first calls I made was to Nana. She and Papa had been praying for me for years, and at last, their prayers had been answered. They rejoiced, spreading the news to family and friends.

Shortly after, my aunt Stacey called. When she told my uncle, he cried. She prayed over me and told me to listen to "Run to the Father" by Cody Carnes. I played it on repeat, letting the lyrics seep into my soul.

Surrender. That's where I was. It was terrifying, yet peaceful. Uncertain, yet sure. For the first time, I knew I was going to be okay. And it made sense why—because for the first time, my soul was saved.

That Sunday, Joe and I attended church with his daughter and her fiancé. I had no idea what to expect.

The moment the music started, I sobbed. I sobbed harder than I had ever sobbed in my life. Worshiping for the first time was unlike anything I had ever experienced. The presence of God filled the room, filled me, and I couldn't contain my emotions.

The weight of my brokenness and disobedience hit me like a train. *What have I done?* And yet, I felt welcome in the church and in the presence of my savior. *This is what truth feels like,* I thought to myself.

Even now, years later, I still cry during worship. Every time, I am reminded of his power, his truth, and his relentless grace. I am reminded of my shortcomings as a human, but that's okay, because it just means I need God, my Creator.

The sermon that day covered Galatians 5, the perfect chapter for where I was.

"The acts of the flesh are obvious: sexual immorality, impurity and debauchery; idolatry and witchcraft; hatred, discord, jealousy, fits of rage, selfish ambition, dissensions, factions and envy; drunkenness, orgies, and the like. I warn you, as I did before, that those who live like this will not inherit the kingdom of God" (Galatians 5:19–21).

I learned that my selfish ambition, something the world had told me was necessary for success, was actually sin. I had spent my entire life chasing things that led only to emptiness, but now, I finally saw what truly mattered.

To this day, it is one of my favorite sections in the Bible because it brought me so much clarity.

Cutting Ties with Darkness

I knew what I had to do. I looked around my apartment at the remnants of my old life. Crystals I had charged under the full moon for "healing energy," sound bowls I used to balance my chakras, tarot and oracle decks I pulled from when I needed "guidance from the universe." I had journals full of affirmations and manifestations written under specific moon phases, astrology books that helped me time decisions or understand my "soul contracts," and a shelf of self-help and spiritual books that told me everything I needed was already inside of me. These things had once brought me a false sense of comfort and control, promising peace, power, or enlightenment, but now they felt empty, even deceptive.

I gathered every last item and got rid of them. I even threw out certain clothes that carried the energy of who I used to be: festival outfits, goddess-themed jewelry, anything that no longer reflected the person I was becoming. This all happened within the span of a few days. I was not messing around.

Then, I turned my attention to Joe. What would happen with us? Would he also give his life to Christ? Should I stay with him? Where would I live? How would I support myself? These questions hung in the air, unanswered. But I would soon find out.

Proposal Under the Eiffel Tower

When I next saw Joe, he told me that if his only purpose in my life had been to lead me to Jesus, then so be it. He claimed he wanted to follow Christ, too.

We picked out an engagement ring together and planned to get married. Meanwhile, we had a trip to Europe booked with my friend Ashley. We went, maintaining my new boundaries (no sex with Joe), and in Paris, under the Eiffel Tower, Joe proposed.

But something felt off.

Throughout the trip, I felt drained. Tired. Like I was forcing something that wasn't meant to be. While in Barcelona, I had one too many drinks by the pool with Ashley and Joe. And in that moment of vulnerability, everything became clear.

That night while we were getting ready to go out, I confided in Ashley that I was having doubts about Joe. Looking back, it seems so obvious. He was a senior citizen, for crying out loud. Plus, I still had feelings for Cody. My heart had never fully healed after our breakup. Ashley reassured me that it wasn't too late to change my mind. She told me to listen to my gut. She seemed relieved that I was finally seeing things more clearly.

That night, I told Joe that I wasn't sure about marriage, that the age gap made me uncomfortable. He was devastated. Angry. But I knew I had to be honest.

I called Nana, telling her everything. She suggested something I had already been considering, that maybe I should move to Ohio and live with her and Papa. I prayed to God to make it obvious to me.

When I broke the news to Joe that I would be leaving, I closed my eyes and saw visions of the forest in Ohio, with deer galloping in the meadow of my grandparents' backyard. That had never happened to me before, despite all of my past visualization techniques I tried so hard to master during my meditations in the past.

Back in California, I packed up my things, broke my lease, and prepared to leave everything behind. I had no income. No clear plan. But I wasn't afraid.

Joe, surprisingly, offered to drive me to Ohio. Our differences became even clearer on the road. By the time we arrived, I was certain this chapter of my life was over.

CLARITY

CHAPTER 9

TRANSFORMATION THROUGH CHRIST

I arrived in Ohio on August 17, 2022, stepping into a world that felt both familiar and foreign. The first thing that struck me was the overwhelming sense of peace. The Midwest has a way of welcoming you home with its open skies and deep-green landscapes. But more than that, my grandparents' home was a refuge. They had acres of land nestled in the woods, and it was a place of stillness, where hummingbirds hovered in golden sunlight and deer wandered freely, unbothered by the chaos of the world.

Nana wasted no time reconnecting me with my extended family. We spent evenings on the deck eating meals infused with love—Papa's grilling, Nana's home-cooked dishes that carried the warmth of my childhood. Their house was always spotless and smelled like nostalgia. It reflected the order and peace that God had given them. But it wasn't just the beauty of nature or the comfort of familiarity that settled my spirit; it was the undeniable presence of God in their home. They were exceptional stewards of what he had given them, and it showed in the way they lived with gratitude, discipline, and love.

I quickly got to work setting up temporary food stamps and Medicaid out of necessity. I was in a place of humility, fully aware that I was someone in need. God was teaching me dependence, stripping away my pride, and showing me that his provision sometimes comes in unexpected ways. I also received unemployment benefits from my corporate job in California, a reminder that even in the wreckage of my past decisions, he was still making a way. I started a part-time nannying job and began Christian therapy. Not exactly where I imagined I'd be at age twenty-seven.

Strengthening Relationships

God's hand was evident in everything. The financial provisions were his blessings. This serene home was his gift. My loving grandparents, new jobs, the church I found, my Christian therapist—each one was a direct extension of his grace and mercy.

New habits began to take root. My mornings started with my Bible, nourishing both soul and body. I worked out, spent time outside, and ended my nights in Scripture. His Word was transforming me from the inside out. Every single night, Nana, Papa, and I would settle into our spots in the living room and open up our Bibles. Nana would pray before Papa would read a Psalm. We all cherished this time with God and each other. They were always there to answer my questions and help guide me deeper into my faith. Their peace was contagious.

I found myself drawn to the Gospels, captivated by Jesus's sacrifices and teachings. The Gospel of Luke, in particular, spoke to me. Luke 9:24 became an anchor: "For whoever wants to save their life will lose it, but whoever loses their life for me will save it." I had spent years clinging to control, desperately trying to shape my own destiny. But the more I surrendered, the more I found freedom. My old life had left me broken. And yet, there in Ohio, in the stillness of God's presence, I was being rebuilt.

Healing and Letting Go of the Past

Despite the healing, my heart still ached for Cody more than I wanted to admit. I tried to bury it, but grief doesn't disappear just because we want it to. I shamelessly reached out to him a few times, hoping to share what Jesus had done in my life. Hoping he would see the light and transformation I had experienced. But he couldn't relate.

It became clear he wasn't reflecting on our relationship the way I was. He wasn't wrestling with conviction or searching for healing the way I was. That realization stung. I wouldn't wish that kind of heartache on anyone. Was this connection I felt just in my head? I continued to pray for him, trusting God to handle what I couldn't.

My days were filled with nannying, working out, reading my Bible, therapy, and church. I was making new friends, but I could feel old relationships slipping away. I realized that not everyone could come with me on this journey.

During this time, God convicted me of past mistakes, leading me to seek forgiveness. Matthew 5:23–24 says: "If you are offering your gift at the altar and there remember that your brother or sister has something against you, leave your gift there in front of the altar. First, go and be reconciled to them; then come and offer your gift." So, I did. I sent messages, apologized to people I had wronged. Most never responded, but that didn't matter. Obedience did.

Dealing with Shame and Guilt

I could physically and mentally feel myself changing and healing from the past. I never thought I would see the day. Almost every day for the previous five years of my life, I had carried deep shame, regret, and embarrassment. The burned bridges haunted my thoughts while I was awake and my dreams while I was asleep.

I couldn't bear the idea that people had a negative image of me in their heads or that I had one of myself. It was all too much. But God and his Word told me to look forward. He had forgiven my sins, so why would I keep holding onto something he had forgotten? "As far as the east is from the west, so far has he removed our transgressions from us" (Psalm 103:12).

The biggest lesson I learned? Without God, it's incredibly difficult to move on from the past, especially when you're weighed down by other people's opinions and perceptions. But with God, I knew he saw it all. He knew my intentions weren't malicious. He saw the pain that fueled some of my worst choices. He also saw the ill intent of others and the wounds they left.

That realization made me see people differently. We all carry pain. We all fall short. It led me to pray for those who hurt me. To this day, I am astonished at the ability God gave me to forgive. To forgive my dad. To forgive Mr. Nelson, Howard, Ted, and Joe for taking advantage of me. I pray for them, genuinely. That's the power of Jesus.

But disentangling from the New Age and my old life wasn't seamless. There were moments I backslid, times when I felt confused or still spiritually entangled. I remember buying a tarot deck, genuinely thinking I could do a "reading" with the Holy Spirit present. I saged my grandparents' house out of habit before realizing what I was inviting in.

Old relational patterns resurfaced too. I was deeply upset at how family members continued to demonize my dad, and I carried the weight of that drama. I had to cut ties with Ashley because she kept pulling me back into an old version of myself, someone who gossiped, said careless things, and couldn't seem to move forward. I dated a few guys on Hinge and had some blurry boundary moments, followed by heavy conviction. I drank too much on a few occasions.

Every time I slipped up, the conviction was immediate, intense, and holy. I couldn't get away with anything, and I say that with deep gratitude. It was as if God had wrapped himself so tightly around me that even in my stumbles, he never let me go. The guilt I felt wasn't from shame or condemnation. It was conviction, paired with a gentle but firm redirection. Before Christ, my sin led to anxiety and self-hatred. But now, even in my weakness, I experienced the kindness of God in sanctification. His discipline wasn't to punish me, it was to protect me. I've never considered walking away from him, not once. I'm his. Permanently. And I'm thankful that even when I struggled, I couldn't deny the presence of the Holy Spirit guiding me back every time.

I decided to download a dating app during my waiting season. I matched with a few men, but I made it clear right away that my faith was most important to me. That helped me quickly weed out the ones who weren't on the same page. One of my matches was someone named Josiah. He came across as really sweet and genuine. For some reason, though, we could never seem to lock down a first date, and eventually, I ghosted him.

Instead, I ended up going on a few dates with another man who was a smooth talker, but in the end, it became clear he

His discipline wasn't

to punish me,

it was to protect me.

wasn't good for me. That experience made me realize it was time to step back, delete the apps, and focus on God for a while longer.

Baptism: A Public Declaration of Faith

I turned twenty-eight with no career, no husband, no close friends, no children, and a broken heart. But I had Jesus. And though I never questioned him, there were nights I lay in bed in agony, overwhelmed by pain from my past. I begged him for relief, and every time, he met me. His presence washed over me like a tidal wave, holding me close as if to say, "I've got you." The depth of his love brought me to tears.

My baptism was the moment everything shifted. I was so eager for it, and when the day finally arrived, I was overwhelmed with joy. I stood alongside others—different ages, different walks of life—all making the same declaration. It was beautiful. We were living proof of redemption.

When I stepped into the water, nothing outwardly miraculous happened. I know baptism is a public declaration of an internal decision and the knowledge that you've been saved. But I can't deny that after my baptism, everything started to change. Every prayer began being answered.

I felt unshakable in my faith. I had embarrassed myself on social media in the past, humiliated myself in ways that haunted me. But this time, there was no shame. No one could humiliate me about my faith because I was sure of it. I wanted people to know that God had changed my life, and I wasn't afraid to share it.

I posted about my baptism. What happened next was nothing short of divine.

New Desires and Divine Appointments

Josiah rarely uses Facebook. He has never messaged a girl after being ghosted by her, and yet, he saw my baptism post and messaged me to congratulate me. What he didn't know was that just days earlier, I had finally let go of Cody. I had written out Bible verses about marriage and the qualities I desired in a husband. I wanted a man with a firm foundation in God who would encourage me. Someone with leadership qualities who would let me help him when he needs it. Someone who was honest, trustworthy, loyal, and committed. I had even drawn a sketch of a couple gazing into each other's eyes, with no idea that God was about to answer that prayer.

But in April 2023, Josiah and I reconnected. Two days before our date, I celebrated my first Easter as a Christian, having recently joined the worship team as a singer. I felt like I was truly finding my voice, and it felt good to use it to glorify God. The sermon that day spoke of redemption—how on Friday, all hope seemed lost, but by Sunday, Jesus had risen, victorious.

Two days later, I got ready for my date with Josiah. I had no expectations. But when I least expected it, God surprised me in ways beyond my imagination.

CHAPTER 10

MATCH MADE IN HEAVEN

When Josiah messaged me after my baptism post, I was a little surprised. It was a simple "congratulations," nothing more. At the time, I was busy lining up interviews for my new career in the hospitality industry, so I didn't think too much of it.

A few days later, I replied to thank him and ask how he was doing. We chatted back and forth and decided to give the date we never went on another chance. We set dinner for Tuesday, April 11, two days after Easter.

We met at a local sushi spot. I arrived first and watched him walk in—his presence instantly filling the space with quiet confidence. My first impression? His muscles. Not gonna lie. We both had a passion for fitness, and I couldn't help but notice.

We introduced ourselves and dove right into conversation, as if we'd known each other for much longer than a few hours.

The conversation flowed easily. We talked about our careers, backgrounds, and faith. I shared a little about my story, unsure how he'd react. But he listened without judgment and was genuinely happy for me. He opened up about his journey in entrepreneurship and all he had built over the years.

We even got to the part where we talked about what we were looking for. No games. No masks. Just honesty. It was so refreshing. We laughed about how polite we were with our sushi, already knowing that in time we'd be scarfing down meals together like maniacs. On that night, though, we were on our best behavior. Three hours flew by.

That night, I came home to a text from him already suggesting ideas for our next date. A man with intention. A man who put effort into us, which was another one of the traits I desired in a man.

Intentional Love

Our next dinner lasted six hours straight. I opened up a little more about my dad, my past, and what I'd been through. I didn't want to scare Josiah off, but I also wasn't going to hide.

I had been "too much" for other men before. But Josiah? He wasn't shaken at all. He embraced me, not despite my past, but because he could see the depth it added to who I was.

As time went on, I shared more because I wanted him to truly know me. I never felt pressured to do so, though. Some of what I'd been through would have made most people run. But when I told Josiah, he looked at me with love and said, "Learning these things about you just makes me love you more. I can see how you seek God and how genuine your faith is."

I'm so grateful that I didn't settle for someone who only loved the good parts of me. I found the one who saw my story through the lens of grace and my walk with God as the most beautiful thing about me.

The Turning Point

On our fourth date, Josiah took me to a painting class. That day, I was feeling extra anxious because another job opportunity had fallen through. But as I sat in his car, a strange peace came over me. I rested my head on his bicep, and for the first time in a while, my heart felt still.

That night, he asked me to be his girlfriend. It was fast, but I already knew. I said yes. The next day, a Sunday, I brought him to church with me.

After service, we went to brunch and laid everything on the table. I told him more about my past and, most importantly, that I had made a commitment: No sex before marriage. Ever again.

This is the point where many women panic. "What if he leaves? What if it ruins things?" But the right man will never be turned off by strong convictions. The right man will breathe a sigh of relief—just like Josiah did.

He told me he had always wanted to be with someone who would stay on the narrow path. In past relationships, he had given into temptation and drifted from God. But now, he had a chance to do things right, and so did I.

Without the weight of sexual sin, we were able to build something real. We spent every moment together getting to know each other deeply, and within a few months, I felt God nudging us toward marriage. It was fast, yes, but when you're both submitted to God, things move at a supernatural pace. During these days, I was often reminded of the truth found in Proverbs 3:5–6: "Trust in the LORD with all your heart and lean not on your own understanding; in all your ways submit to him, and he will make your paths straight."

At the same time, another dream came to life. After a year of trusting God, I had landed my dream job as a business travel sales manager at a high-end hotel in Cleveland. Everything was falling into place.

The Wedding We Didn't Plan

Meeting Josiah's family only confirmed what I already assumed. His parents were warm, grounded, and welcoming. So very different from the parents of guys I had dated before.

Josiah had spent years without a girlfriend, choosing to focus on his work and building financial security for the family he prayed for. That's the kind of man worth waiting for, one led by God, not led by impulse.

Just two months into dating, he proposed. It was June. He was thirty-one, I was twenty-eight. We knew what we wanted, and we had waited long enough. We started planning a small wedding. We toured venues, explored options, but one day, I looked at him and said, "Ugh, this is so much work. What if we just saved the money and eloped in Hawaii instead?"

"Um, you read my mind," he replied. "And we'll have an epic honeymoon."

So that's exactly what we did.

Kauaʻi: A Vow, a Beach, and God's Presence

It was the middle of August, and the weather in Kauaʻi was perfect. Josiah and I had flown there with a few hiccups along the way, including delayed flights, a flat tire on the plane, and missed layovers. But in the end, the chaos turned into blessings. We received vouchers and even got upgraded to first class when the airline found out we were getting married. We were on cloud nine. As I looked out the plane window, I felt like my dream was coming true.

Landing in Kauaʻi, I couldn't help but tell Josiah I wanted to move there. The island is the most rural of all the Hawaiian islands, full of beautiful views, wild chickens, friendly people, quaint little shops, and hole-in-the-wall restaurants with the best poke I've ever tasted. With the delays, we barely had time to breathe before rushing to our hair and wedding appointments. Our ceremony happened mere hours after we landed!

I slipped into my dress, a lacy, beachy Free People number, my hair in a low updo with a matching bow to keep the beach wind at bay. I met Josiah on the beach, and we exchanged vows we had written ourselves. I'll never forget the tears streaming down his cheeks as he spoke, telling me he had waited for the right girl for so long and that it had been worth the wait. In that moment, I felt the beauty of God's timing. Waiting wasn't wasted, and surrendering to his plan brought something far better than I could have orchestrated on my own.

We captured photos along Kauaʻi's cliffs, then celebrated with a sushi dinner before collapsing from exhaustion. With the six-hour time change, we were up at 5 a.m. the next morning, rushing to the resort gym, checking out hot tubs, and watching the sunrise on the beach and having a sunrise photoshoot. And that's when our honeymoon truly began.

We hiked to waterfalls, took a boat tour along the Nā Pali Coast, soared in a helicopter with the doors off, cliff-jumped, ate incredible food, and explored the entire island together. Everywhere I looked—the waves, the wind, the birds—I felt beauty beyond belief. I even caught sight of little babies and prayed that one day soon we would have one of our own.

I felt peaceful, excited, full of joy and awe. God's presence was palpable in every moment, and I knew deep down that this trip would forever hold a special place in our hearts. Looking back, I realize it wasn't just a honeymoon; it was a celebration of patience, faith, and the blessings that come when you trust God's timing completely.

CHAPTER 11

LEAVING THE WORLD BEHIND

The first few months of marriage were sweet in many ways, but they didn't feel fully peaceful. Something was stealing my joy, and it was my job.

I had worked so hard to earn a management position in the hospitality industry, especially since I had no previous experience in that field. On paper, it looked like a win. But the reality was far from what I'd imagined. The commute alone was forty-five minutes each way, and instead of a typical nine to five, it was more like eight to five with an unspoken expectation to arrive early and stay late. The irony was, there wasn't even enough work to fill half of those hours. I spent entire days alone in my office, scrolling social media to pass the time, while also feeling the constant pressure to look busy.

When I did go above and beyond, it was met with criticism, not appreciation. I asked to work from home one day a week and was immediately shut down. It was a toxic combination of boredom, surveillance, and burnout. Corporate life felt like a cage to me. I don't thrive in rigid boxes. I think big, move fast, and feel deeply.

But in that world, any spark of life felt threatening to people just trying to survive.

I would sit in that office daydreaming: What if I could just be home? I imagined bringing life and beauty into our house. Josiah's 100-year-old bachelor pad desperately needed a woman's touch. I pictured cooking dinner, staying consistent with workouts, creating content, and sharing my story. I imagined finally taking social media seriously—as a tool for purpose instead of vanity.

But more than any of that, I felt a pull I couldn't shake.

I wanted to become a mother.

Goodbye, Nine to Five

Josiah and I had originally talked about enjoying our first year of marriage before starting a family. But the thought of waiting didn't feel right. I had already felt uncomfortable with birth control; the side effects scared me, and something in my spirit felt off about it. After some honest conversations, we decided to try for a baby. It took a little time for Josiah to get there, but once he did, he was all in.

I began praying seriously about what it would look like to leave my job. I wasn't pregnant yet. We didn't have a full plan. But I knew God was speaking to me. I also knew my husband was a faithful provider. And most of all, I knew I had to trust.

So, I quit.

And not even a month later, I found out I was pregnant.

I couldn't believe it. After everything I had put my body through— the stress, the mistreatment, the sin—I was terrified I wouldn't be able to conceive. I had believed the lie that I would be punished for my past. But God doesn't operate like that. His mercy is greater than my mistakes.

Letting go of my career ambitions, my independence, and my "girl boss" mindset wasn't easy. The world had trained me to place my worth in titles, productivity, and independence. But God was calling me to place my worth in *him*.

It was a turning point. I was no longer chasing applause. I was learning to live in obedience.

Redefining Success

I wish I could tell you that after I quit my job, things fell into place, that I finally found my groove on social media, built a thriving community, and turned my story into a career that helped provide for our family. I pictured it so clearly: women being inspired by my posts, lives being changed, fruit growing from my obedience.

But that's not what happened.

In the two years since I quit my job, I've seen very little traction on my social media platforms. I've struggled with consistency, direction, and confidence. There have been moments I've wondered, *Did I hear God wrong?* Or maybe it's just not his timing yet.

But deep down, I'm learning this: Obedience doesn't always look like immediate fruit. And success in God's kingdom often looks like faithfulness, not followers.

Would it be helpful to have a platform that earns money and spreads my message? Sure. But the truth is, we don't need it. We have more than enough.

And even if the numbers are low, my story has *still* helped people. Not through viral posts or flashy reels, but through quiet DMs and vulnerable conversations. That counts.

I'm also realizing something about myself: I'm more comfortable writing than being on camera. I haven't figured out how to be fully *me* on social media yet. It's something I want to grow in, and maybe this book is the beginning of that.

And maybe—just maybe—the story I thought I wanted isn't the story God is writing.

Just like he changed my heart about motherhood, about being a wife, about control and striving and success, maybe he's changing this desire, too.

Not because I gave up. But because I'm waking up.

Leaving the world behind wasn't a one-time decision. It's a daily choice to surrender what I thought I needed and receive what he knows I do.

Sacred Motherhood

This may sound vain, but the first thing I wrote when I sat down to reflect on pregnancy was: No one can really prepare you to gain fifty pounds. I didn't reflect on the fluttering kicks or the emotional high of gender reveal day. Not the joy of my baby shower, which was one of the best days of my life, or even the sacred privilege of being chosen to grow a human inside of me. All of that was real and beautiful.

And still, pregnancy was one of the hardest things I've ever done.

I love motherhood so much that I want more babies. But being pregnant? That's a different story. I have hope that the second time around will be easier, but there's something about being pregnant for the first time that's like, *Wait, WHAT is happening to my body?*

The first trimester? I was so tired I could barely function. The second? A dream—cute bump, glowing skin, nesting mode in full swing. The third? Just a big, uncomfortable waiting game full of back pain, swelling, and constant anxiety about what labor would be like.

That's the thing about pregnancy that no one talks about enough: It's the death of control. You can't control how your body changes. You can't control when the baby comes. You can't control how you'll feel from one day to the next. You just have to *surrender.* You heal. You build. You fight. You pray. And more than ever, you learn to lean—on God, your husband, your support system, your faith. It feels like you're not doing enough, and yet you're doing the most sacred work in the world. As my belly grew, so did my understanding of God's design for motherhood. It is not a backup plan. It is not a lesser calling. It is a divine assignment.

The enemy tries to convince women that raising children is small and insignificant. That if you're not earning money or chasing a dream, your life doesn't count. But motherhood isn't small. It's generational warfare. The love, wisdom, and faith we pour into our children will outlive any career milestone.

I realized I didn't need to chase after an identity I had already surrendered. I didn't need to hustle for validation. I had been entrusted with a child—and the gift of being fully present in her life from the very beginning. I refused to take that for granted. Being a mother is indescribable. It just keeps getting better every day.

The love I have for Aurora literally astounds me. She loves me so purely, it breaks me open in the best way. And watching Josiah love her, seeing her love him back, and us all loving each other—it's just one big mushy love story that I never want to end.

So, bring on the cheese. Because this life, this calling, this family—it's bliss.

It's everything I didn't know I needed.

And it's all because I said yes to God.

Greatest Blessing

This journey has taught me that God's plan really is better than mine. Even when I was scared to quit my job, look at what he did. He blessed us with a pregnancy, he allowed me to retire at a young age, he gave me the honor of staying home with our daughter. We can spend our lives chasing our own plans, or we can surrender and walk in his. And when we do? He blesses us in ways we never could have imagined. The fruit of surrender is not always flashy, public, or praised by the world. But it's real, eternal, and worth everything.

One time as I held my daughter in my arms, I couldn't help but grieve over all the lies I once believed about womanhood, power, and freedom. The lies that told me my value was in my image, that motherhood was a burden, and that I needed to follow "my truth" instead of *the* truth.

I had spent years unknowingly trapped in spiritual deception, pulling from New Age practices, manifesting self-centered dreams, and embracing a false sense of empowerment. And I wasn't the only one. These lies are everywhere.

Now that I had tasted the real thing—real love, real truth, real fruit—I couldn't stay silent. If even one woman sees the truth and turns to Jesus, then it's worth it all.

CHAPTER 12

CALL TO REDEMPTION

t feels surreal to look back on who I used to be, because I really don't recognize that person anymore. I was once a broken, abused, shattered, and dysfunctional human. I was defiant, rebellious, and prideful. I lacked self-awareness and truth. I was deceived. But God met me in my brokenness. He opened my eyes to see and gave me a new heart: "I will give you a new heart and put a new spirit in you; I will remove from you your heart of stone and give you a heart of flesh" (Ezekiel 36:26).

God softened my hardened heart, allowing true transformation and healing to take place not for my own glory, but for his. Through complete surrender and obedience to him, I found marriage, motherhood, peace, and true purpose. Healing is a journey, and God continues to refine me daily, chiseling away at the things that do not align with him.

Following God has been the most humbling experience of my life. My heart is on fire for him, and I want to change and be better. But sanctification is a process. I am constantly being shown ways I can soften my heart and surrender my flaws. The difference now is I don't avoid corrections. I don't shame myself, twist the truth, or justify my behavior like I used to.

God's corrections are gentle. When he reveals an area I need to grow in, I'm open to it, even when it's hard. Some flaws are deeply ingrained, shaped by a lifetime of being one way. But reading his Word helps clarify what's wise and acceptable in his eyes.

The Book of Proverbs, for example, reveals the path of wisdom and calls out what leads to destruction. You don't instantly become perfect when you give your life to Christ, though sometimes people assume that's what you think you are. And it's not easy, especially when you start going against the grain of culture.

Still, the beautiful thing about being saved is that no one else can tell you who you are anymore. The only approval you care about is God's. His truth becomes the standard. His love is freeing, even when others think your obedience is limiting.

I don't avoid certain things because I'm controlled. I avoid them because I love God, respect myself, and my soul just won't allow certain compromises anymore. The music I listen to, the things I watch, the words I use, the people I surround myself with—everything has shifted.

I no longer practice yoga. Even though it made me feel strong and graceful, I let it go because life without it—life with Jesus—is so much better. I no longer swear, even when it might feel humorous or relatable. Those words do not honor God. I've stopped listening to some of my favorite artists because their messages disturb my peace. I barely watch anything on TV anymore because so much of what's out there is sick, dark, and spiritually harmful.

If it doesn't honor God, I stay away from it.

Never Beyond God's Grace

If you feel stuck in your past, if you can't seem to move forward without replaying your mistakes, decisions, or the pain of a relationship that ended badly, I am here to tell you that you can be redeemed. You are not too far gone. No mistake, no sin, no failure is beyond God's grace.

God's Word is proof of this. Take Paul, for example. Before his radical transformation, he was Saul of Tarsus, a man who persecuted Christians, hunted them down, and approved of their deaths. He was the very enemy of Christ's followers. But then, Jesus met him on the road to Damascus, and everything changed (Acts 9). The very man who once sought to destroy the church became one of its greatest apostles, writing much of the New Testament and spreading the gospel to the ends of the earth.

If God could redeem Paul, he can redeem you. He can redeem that person in your life that seems like they will never find the light.

This is the power of God's restoration. He not only forgives but also restores and repurposes what was lost. Joel 2:25 declares: "I will restore to you the years that the swarming locust has eaten" (ESV).

Think about that for a moment. God doesn't just forgive; he restores. He brings beauty from ashes. He takes what the enemy meant for harm and turns it for good (Genesis 50:20). He rewrites our stories, making them testimonies that glorify him.

Maybe you're thinking, *But my past is different. I haven't done anything particularly bad compared to others.* The truth is, even if you've lived a morally good life by the world's standards, you still need redemption.

You are not too far gone. No mistake, no sin, no failure is beyond God's grace.

Romans 3:10 says: "There is no one righteous, not even one." And Romans 3:23 reminds us: "For all have sinned and fall short of the glory of God."

No one is exempt from needing a savior. Whether our sins seem big or small, we all fall short, and we all need Jesus. Redemption is not about what we have done; it is about what he has done. It is through Christ alone that we are made new: "Therefore, if anyone is in Christ, he is a new creation. The old has passed away; behold, the new has come" (2 Corinthians 5:17 ESV).

This is the beauty of redemption. We are not defined by our past but by who we become in Christ. When we surrender our lives to him, we don't just get a fresh start, we are made entirely new.

So, if you're carrying shame, if you feel unworthy, if you believe you've gone too far, know this: Jesus is calling you. He is waiting with open arms, ready to redeem, restore, and rewrite your story.

You don't have to stay where you are. You don't have to live in regret.

All you have to do is say yes to him.

But saying yes to Jesus is not about getting your life in perfect order first. It's not about cleaning yourself up before you come to him. You come as you are, and he is the one who makes you clean.

He is not afraid of your mess.

He is not intimidated by your doubts.

He is not disgusted by your sin.

He already paid the price.

The enemy wants you to believe that it's too late. That you've made too many mistakes. That you've missed your shot at a meaningful life. But that is a lie from the pit of hell. As long as you are breathing, it is not too late.

Redemption is not just a one-time decision; it's a new way of living. It's the decision to take off the mask, stop performing, and step into the truth. It's trusting that Jesus really did die for your sins, and that he rose again so you could have new life—real life—in him.

Maybe you've known *of* Jesus your whole life, but you've never fully surrendered to him. Maybe you've walked away from your faith and wondered if you could ever come back. Maybe you're just now realizing the weight of your sin and your desperate need for a savior.

Whoever you are, you are not reading this by accident. Jesus is calling you. He is not offering religion; he's offering relationship. He is not offering rules; he's offering redemption. He is not offering empty promises; he's offering eternal life. Let him in. There's no sin he cannot forgive. There's no past he cannot redeem. There's no heart too broken for him to heal. This is the call to redemption, and it is for you.

Facing the Consequences

When I look back on my past, I see so many choices. Some came from deception, some from rebellion against God, some from my mental health struggles or trauma, and some from plain selfishness. Whatever the reason, the truth is that I still live with the consequences. Even though God has rescued me and made me new, I don't get to erase the past.

Some days it feels like my memories sneak up out of nowhere. A certain smell, a song, a random moment, and suddenly I'm reliving something I thought I had buried. Those memories leave me helpless, angry with myself, or even upset with others who were part of it. I can't sweep them away. That's part of the struggle—I live forgiven, but not forgetful.

Sometimes during this refining process, I forget who I am in Christ. I regress back into old thought patterns. I feel hopeless.

> That's part of
> the struggle—
> I live forgiven,
> but not forgetful.

Sometimes that hopelessness makes me cling to God tighter than ever before. Other times, I look for distractions. I scroll on social media or numb myself in little ways that only make things worse. But every time, on the other side of the fire, I come out remembering who I am in God. And I truly believe that, even though it's hard, I'm being made better for it.

Still, there are days I fear I'll be haunted by my past forever. My inner voice can sound like my father's voice, the one that used to tell me I was selfish, attention-seeking, stupid, or bad. Those words stuck, and even today, they echo in my head when I'm at my weakest. The difference is that now I have the discernment to recognize where those lies come from. They're not God's voice. They're not my true identity. That realization makes me pray—for myself, for my family, and even for my dad. Because I know he carries wounds of his own, and I wouldn't wish the cycle of hurt on my worst enemy.

God hears those prayers. He hears the cries from the places we don't show anyone else. Scripture tells us, "Do not conform to the pattern of this world, but be transformed by the renewing of your mind" (Romans 12:2). That transformation isn't instant. It's daily. Sometimes it feels like two steps forward, one step back. But even in the setbacks, God is at work.

Malachi says God "will sit as a refiner and purifier of silver" (v. 3:3). When silver is refined, it has to be heated by fire until the impurities rise to the surface and can be removed. The silversmith knows the silver is ready when he can see his reflection in it. That's what God does with me. Every consequence, every memory I wish I could erase, every piece of my past that I'd rather forget, he uses like fire, burning away what doesn't belong, until my life reflects him more clearly.

And maybe that's why I feel led to share all this with you. Because if you're struggling, I want you to know you aren't alone. Even surrounded by blessings—a loving husband, a beautiful daughter, and supportive people around me—I've still felt the ache of loneliness. I've still battled shame and negative self-talk. But through it all, God has never let me go.

So, if you've ever wondered whether you'll always feel this way, whether you'll always be haunted by the past or weighed down by your own thoughts, I want you to know there is hope. God is refining you like silver. He's not wasting your fire. You are not your past. You are not the voices of others. You are his.

"Forget the former things; do not dwell on the past. See, I am doing a new thing! Now it springs up; do you not perceive it?" (Isaiah 43:18–19).

CHAPTER 13

BOLD FAITH IN A WORLD THAT OPPOSES IT

If you're a new Christian and not married, here's my heartfelt advice: Go celibate. Start praying and thinking about the kind of spouse you want, one who honors God and respects you. Don't have sex until you're married. Sex outside of marriage will taint your soul and damage your heart in ways I can't emphasize enough.

Get a Bible. Read it daily. Pray constantly. Weed out toxic people—not from spite, but to make room for true community and discipleship.

In a world that increasingly opposes Jesus, many Christians are shrinking back. They're afraid to speak the truth, afraid of being mocked or misunderstood. But this opposition isn't new.

In Jesus's time, people rejected him, too. The Pharisees and religious leaders couldn't handle the truth he brought because it exposed their sin and pride. They mocked him, called him a deceiver, even claimed he was demon-possessed (John 7). They hated the truth because it demanded change.

That hasn't changed. People still reject truth because accepting it requires humility and surrender. They would rather deny God than confront their brokenness.

I've faced judgment, too—receiving hate-filled comments, being called schizophrenic for believing in God, and being told that I made him up just to survive life. At first, those comments made me angry. I wanted to clap back. But God softened my response. He helped me see the hurt behind the words.

Now, I choose to respond with grace or sometimes not at all. Proverbs 26:4 says, "Do not answer a fool according to his folly, or you yourself will be just like him." Some arguments are not worth your energy.

Our job isn't to convince those who won't listen, but to share the gospel so that as many people as possible will join God's kingdom and to stay faithful and let God do the work in people's hearts. Romans 1:16 says, "For I am not ashamed of the gospel, because it is the power of God that brings salvation to everyone who believes." We must be bold, even if it costs us something. The world may oppose us, but we are never alone. God is with us, and his truth always prevails.

When You're Confused About Your Purpose

We all crave direction. We want to know our calling, our mission, the "why" behind our lives. And when we don't see it clearly, we feel stuck or afraid we've missed it.

But God is not a God of confusion (1 Corinthians 14:33). He promises to direct our steps if we trust him fully (Proverbs 3:5–6). The hard part is we want clarity *now*. We want the full plan, all laid out. But God often leads one step at a time, teaching us trust, patience, and surrender along the way.

If you feel lost, here are some promises to hold onto:

- "'For I know the plans I have for you,' declares the LORD . . ." (Jeremiah 29:11).
- "The LORD will fight for you; you need only to be still" (Exodus 14:14).
- "Commit your work to the LORD, and your plans will be established" (Proverbs 16:3 ESV).
- "We know that in all things God works for the good of those who love him..." (Romans 8:28).
- "Delight yourself in the LORD, and he will give you the desires of your heart" (Psalm 37:4 ESV).

These truths don't just comfort, they anchor you.

Worldly Ambition vs. Godly Purpose

The world tells us to chase success—more money, more followers, more everything. But the more we chase, the emptier we often feel.

Think about something you desperately wanted in the past. Now that you have it, did it satisfy you for long? Or are you already on to the next goal?

Galatians 5:26 warns us: "Let us not become conceited, provoking one another, envying one another" (ESV). Worldly ambition is never satisfied, but godly purpose fills your soul.

God has redirected my life over and over again. And it's not always easy. I still battle restlessness, comparison, and fleshly desires. I still have to pray for grounding when I feel tempted to seek validation or success in the world's eyes.

This isn't a one-time lesson. It's daily. A daily dying to the flesh. A daily yes to God. But that yes leads to peace, and peace is priceless.

If a Loved One Is Lost

Chances are, someone you love has a heart that feels hardened toward Jesus. Maybe they've been deceived by the media, the school system, or even by a church or family environment that misrepresented him. Maybe they've gone through deep trauma or abuse. Or maybe you simply don't know what happened. Whatever the reason, it is heartbreaking to watch someone you love reject the salvation, peace, and love of Jesus, especially when you know what that means for their eternity.

The one thing that has brought me peace is remembering this: God loves them more than I do. He longs for them to come to him even more than I long for it. He is always working in ways we cannot see, and his heart is patient, merciful, and full of love.

So, what do we do in the meantime? We pray.

I am convinced that one of the biggest reasons God saved me out of the New Age deception was because of the faithful prayers of my grandparents, my aunts and uncles, and their church friends who carried me into their Bible studies and prayer groups. They knew the power of prayer. I believe their intercession was a shield around me, and even the destruction I kept running into was God's mercy in response to their prayers, frustrating my attempts to succeed without him. I often wondered why I could never seem to "make it" in the world's way, and now I believe it's because no force of darkness can overcome the power of Jesus's name spoken in prayer.

So, never stop praying. But when you pray, release the responsibility of being the one who has to save them. Salvation is God's work, not yours. He hears your prayers. He is working on their heart. And as you intercede for them, don't neglect to also ask him to shape you, to give you wisdom, and to refine your own walk with him.

There are still many people in my family who are not yet saved. If I carried the full weight of that, it would crush me. Instead, I daily place them in God's hands. That's where they belong.

I want to invite you now to do the same, and to pray with me for your loved ones who do not yet know Jesus:

Prayer for Unsaved Loved Ones

Father, we praise you and thank you for salvation through your Son, Jesus Christ. We thank you that you are merciful, patient, and full of love. Lord, you see our loved ones who are far from you. You know their hurts, their doubts, their wounds, and the lies that hold them captive. We lift them up to you today.

Father, break through the hardness of their hearts. Remove every deception and open their eyes to see the truth of who you are. Draw them to Jesus by the power of your Spirit. Protect them from the enemy's schemes, and place people in their path who will speak your Word with love and boldness.

Lord, give us endurance in prayer. Help us to trust that you are working, even when we cannot see it. Guard us from fear, discouragement, or taking on a burden that belongs only to you. Shape us, refine us, and let our lives reflect your love so they may see Christ in us.

We believe in the power of Jesus's name, and we declare it over our loved ones. May every chain be broken, every lie silenced, and every wandering heart come home to you.

In the mighty name of Jesus we pray,
Amen.

Remember to Pray for Those Who Have Hurt You

The world tells us to "ghost," "cut off access," or "get even." But Jesus calls us to something radically different: "If you forgive those who sin against you, your heavenly Father will forgive you. But if you refuse to forgive others, your Father will not forgive your sins" (Matthew 6:14–15 NLT).

Not only does Jesus teach us to forgive, but he makes it clear that our very lives and eternity depend on it. Forgiveness is not optional for the believer. It is the evidence that we have received God's forgiveness ourselves.

Jesus takes it even further: "But I say to you, love your enemies, bless those who curse you, do good to those who hate you, and pray for those who spitefully use you and persecute you" (Matthew 5:44 NKJV).

This is not natural to us. It takes the strength of the Holy Spirit to pray for those who have wounded us. Yet, when we do, our hearts begin to heal, and we reflect the very heart of Christ on the cross: "Father, forgive them, for they do not know what they are doing" (Luke 23:34).

Now, forgiveness does not mean you allow continual abuse, manipulation, or unrepentant sin into your life. Boundaries are biblical and wise. Some people are not meant to remain in close relationship with you, especially if they refuse to acknowledge their wrongdoing or continue to harm you. You can forgive someone completely while still keeping necessary distance.

But here is the warning: Don't allow bitterness, anger, or hatred to take root in your heart. God sees the heart, and he knows when unforgiveness lingers.

In a culture that glorifies cutting people off at the first mistake, I want to challenge you: Go to God in prayer. If someone is sincerely repentant and showing fruit of change, don't dismiss them so quickly. Extend the same grace you yourself have received from Christ.

I'll be honest, there are bridges I've burned that I wish could be rebuilt. Some of those relationships may never be restored, and that's okay. My responsibility is not to control the outcome; it's to obey God. I can forgive, release the weight of bitterness, and keep praying for them.

And when you pray for those who hurt you, remember this: Sometimes people cannot love you because they do not know the love of the Father. They cannot give what they do not have. That's why they need your prayers. Pray for their healing. Pray for their salvation. Pray that one day they will encounter the transforming love of Jesus Christ.

The Way of Surrender

I often remind myself to look at how far God has brought me in just three years. There is no denying that there is no other explanation besides God. Every single thing I tried before surrendering my life to Jesus ended in destruction. My mental illness, my alcohol use, my trauma, my substance abuse, my sexual immorality, my New Age practices, my career—every pursuit, every attempt to fix myself with my own strength—failed. But the moment I changed directions, the moment I made a 180-degree turn and radically devoted my life to Jesus, my life changed too.

Blessing after blessing, I watched as he revealed my true purpose, aligning my heart with his. He healed what I thought was beyond repair. He made beauty from the ashes of my past. And now, here I am, alive to speak about it, to tell you that the same redemption is possible for you. Not by your own strength, not by self-improvement or good deeds, but by his grace and power alone.

Wherever you are in your journey, God is calling you to him. Let me be absolutely clear when I say this: Redemption is possible for *anyone* through Jesus Christ, but it is *only* possible through Jesus Christ.

As we come to the close of this journey, I want to leave you with one thing: You are not beyond redemption. No matter where you've been, what you've done, or how lost you may feel, there is a call on your life that only God can fulfill.

This is the moment to take a step, even if it's a small one. The first step toward freedom, toward healing, and toward purpose is always surrender. Surrender to the One who loves you unconditionally, who has always been waiting for you to come home.

> Redemption is possible for *anyone* through Jesus Christ, but it is *only* possible through Jesus Christ.

It's not about having it all together. It's about being willing to admit that you can't do it on your own and that you need a savior. This chapter is for you to reflect on everything we've covered and to make the choice to step into the fullness of what God has for you.

If you're ready to surrender, I want to guide you through this moment with a prayer, one that you can say your own. Take your time, let these words resonate, and allow God to meet you right where you are.

Prayer of Surrender

God, I come before you today with an open heart. I recognize that I am a sinner, and I cannot save myself. I believe that Jesus Christ died for my sins and rose again, offering me forgiveness and eternal life. I ask you to forgive me for my mistakes, my wrong choices, and my rebellion against you.

I surrender my life to you, Lord. Take away my past, my pride, and my fear. Make me new. I want to live for you and walk in your truth. Help me to trust you every day, to follow your Word, and to live out your purpose for my life.

Fill me with your Holy Spirit and give me the strength to follow you boldly. I choose you, Jesus. Lead me on this journey of redemption. In Jesus's name, Amen.

Your Surrender

Now, I encourage you to take a moment to write down your own surrender to God. What are you letting go of? What are you trusting God with today? There is power in putting pen to paper and making this decision personal. Take your time to reflect and write down what God is calling you to.

I MANIFESTED MY WORST NIGHTMARE

EPILOGUE

cradle my daughter in my arms, gently rocking her as she drifts off for her first nap of the day. The soft morning light filters through the window, casting a warm glow over the room. As I hum a worship song, my voice cracking but full of praise, I lift one hand high, closing my eyes as tears well up. At this moment, I am overwhelmed with gratitude. It is nothing short of a miracle that this is my life.

If you had told me three years ago that I'd be here, married to a man who loves me, feeling safe, stable, and provided for so I could stay home with our baby and live a soft life, free to focus on my passions, I would have laughed in your face. If you had told me that my unhealthy ambition to become a famous singer, actress, or billionaire entrepreneur would dissolve, that I would no longer be desperately climbing the corporate ladder, I would have thought you were crazy. And if you had told me that I, the proud feminist girl boss, would one day call Jesus Christ my Lord and Savior, I would have told you that you were absolutely nuts.

There may be people reading this who knew me, knew of me, or who were mentioned in this story. In the off chance that you are reading this and recognize yourself, I want you to know that I've changed names and details out of respect for your privacy. My purpose in sharing these stories is not to point fingers, but to share my own journey, of how things unfolded and what I've learned, all to the glory of God.

I hold no bitterness toward anyone mentioned. In fact, I grieve over the pain and confusion I may have caused. I've come to see how powerful and freeing true forgiveness is, not just for others, but for myself. In Christ, I've found a worth that can't be shaken by my past and a hope that's bigger than anything I've been through. That's the message I pray reaches you too.

Since becoming a Christian, my heart toward my parents, and really my whole family, has only softened. Although my relationship with my dad has been pretty nonexistent for some time now, I still think back on the good times we had with genuine fondness. I remember the funny quirks, the adventures, and the stories that used to make me laugh. I love him, and that love has not changed. I trust that God is not done writing our story and that he's already working in ways I can't yet see.

That doesn't take away from where others in my family are in their healing journey. I recognize everyone's experience is unique, but I can only speak for myself. I hold no bitterness, only hope. My deepest desire is that every person in my family finds the peace, purpose, and freedom that can only come from surrendering their life to Jesus.

I love each of them, and I continue to pray that they come to know the truth of who he is.

APPENDIX A

THE HIDDEN ROOTS OF NEW AGE PRACTICES: A PERSONAL GLOSSARY OF DECEPTION

A s you've read in my story, I became deeply involved in many New Age practices during my search for healing, purpose, and truth. What I didn't realize at the time was that these seemingly harmless or even "spiritual" tools were actually opening doors to deception and darkness.

The New Age is not just a trendy lifestyle or vague belief system. It's a carefully disguised counterfeit to the truth of God. Many of its practices come from ancient pagan religions, Eastern mysticism, and occult teachings. They promise enlightenment, healing, empowerment, and self-discovery, but they lead people further from the true God and deeper into spiritual confusion. The most dangerous part is that for decades, even centuries, these deceptions have been woven into our education system, media, pop culture, and daily lives, making them feel normal and easy to fall into without question.

This appendix breaks down many of the New Age practices I personally engaged in. For each one, I'll explain what it is, why it's appealing, what's really behind it, and what the Bible says.

My prayer is that this serves as a helpful reference, especially if you're unsure about something you've been practicing, or if someone you love is caught up in these beliefs. I don't share this to condemn anyone. I was once there too. I share this to warn, equip, and shine light on what the enemy doesn't want you to see.

You don't have to stay confused. God's Word is clear. When you start comparing New Age teachings to the Bible, the truth becomes undeniable: These practices lead away from Jesus, not toward him.

If you're currently involved in the New Age movement, please know that I'm not here to judge. Honestly, before I met Jesus if I had come across someone warning about how dangerous New Age thinking is, I probably would have felt defensive. But when people shared small pieces of truth with me, it planted seeds that eventually helped me. That's my heart behind this chapter. I want to share truth in hopes it will do the same for you.

What Is the New Age?

The New Age is difficult to pin down because, by nature, it resists being defined. It isn't one unified belief system but rather a collection of practices and ideas that promise inner peace, self-discovery, and spiritual awakening. The common thread is the pursuit of a "higher consciousness," the idea that when enough individuals look inward, transcend, and awaken, the world itself will shift into harmony and become a better place.

Because the focus is on individuality and self-realization, the New Age typically rejects the idea of one governing higher power. Instead, it teaches that divinity is within us, waiting to be uncovered or awakened. But as many of us have come to see, true peace, truth, and transformation are found only in Jesus Christ, not in ourselves.

Yoga and Meditation

As I discussed in Chapter 4, some people mistakenly believe that yoga is only a physical practice or philosophy, but in my training course to become an instructor, I was taught that it is a religion. While yoga is often presented as a tool for flexibility, fitness, or stress relief, its roots go much deeper. Yoga originated in ancient India as a spiritual discipline within Hinduism. The physical postures (*asanas*), breathing techniques (*pranayama*), and meditation practices were designed to awaken a spiritual energy called *kundalini*, with the goal of achieving unity with the divine—not the God of the Bible, but a false version of divinity rooted in pantheism and self-worship.

Each pose and sequence in yoga is connected to a specific deity or divine energy, whether people realize it or not. For example, dancer's pose (*natarajasana*) bows to Lord Shiva, depicted as the cosmic dancer Nataraja, embodying universal bliss and grace. Practicing this pose links the practitioner to Shiva's cosmic dance of creation, preservation, and destruction, a symbolic "dance of bliss" representing the eternal rhythm of the universe. Even the popular sun salutation is an act of bowing to the sun. Because these movements are inseparable from their spiritual origins, it's impossible to truly practice yoga as "just exercise," and this challenges the notion that Christians can safely engage in it without spiritual compromise.

Meditation, as taught in New Age spirituality, or in its more secular form, "mindfulness," isn't about prayer or seeking God. It's about emptying your mind, focusing on the breath, or aligning with your "higher self." Even when stripped of all the New Age language, the goal is the same: creating an empty mental space. While it might feel peaceful or empowering at first, this practice can open the door to spiritual influences that are not from God. By intentionally emptying your mind, you create a spiritual vacuum—and something will fill it. This makes your mind an easy stomping ground for the enemy, even for those who don't consider themselves spiritual.

God's design for meditation is completely different. He calls us to meditate on his Word, to dwell on his truth, and to let his Spirit guide our thoughts. True peace, clarity, and transformation come not from emptying our minds, but from filling them with God's presence, promises, and wisdom.

Yoga and meditation are appealing because they're marketed as self-care and healing. They're trendy, accessible, and heavily endorsed by therapists, influencers, and celebrities. And in a world full of anxiety and noise, who wouldn't want to feel peace and calm? But that's the hook. The peace feels real, but it doesn't last. And if it doesn't come from Jesus, it's not true peace.

The truth is, yoga is not simply stretching. It's a spiritual practice deeply rooted in Eastern mysticism. Every pose was designed to honor Hindu gods, and the overall goal is to awaken spiritual power *without* God. As for meditation, the Bible never tells us to empty our minds but to renew them, and to take every thought captive in obedience to Christ (2 Corinthians 10:5). When we remove God from the picture, we make ourselves vulnerable to deception.

Yoga was the very first practice that snowballed me into the world of spirituality. I had my spiritual awakening during a yoga class, and I now look back on it as the "gateway" into all the other New Age practices I eventually embraced. It all stemmed from yoga. At first, I turned to yoga to help me cope with anxiety and body image issues. It felt like a healthy outlet, and I became completely obsessed with it. I truly felt like I had found my life's calling. But the deeper I got, the more I noticed how it was mixed with spiritual language, such as chants, mantras, and talk of "energy" and aligning with the "universe." I started practicing guided meditations and breathwork, believing I was connecting to peace. But I wasn't connecting to God.

Instead, I became more spiritually sensitive but also more confused. I opened doors I didn't even realize were dangerous, smoking weed while I practiced to feel even more euphoric, practicing alongside my crystals for extra healing, journaling manifestations, or doing poses under the full moon. Deception always looks like light at first. I didn't understand back then that peace without Christ is a counterfeit. It fades fast, and it can leave you even more empty than before. All in all, God used my experience with yoga for good. Through it, he opened my eyes to the truth, and now I can share what I've learned to help others. I don't necessarily regret that season because it served an important purpose in my life, but that doesn't mean I would recommend it to anyone. Learn from my experience, and spare yourself the spiritual deception.

Scripture to Expose Deception:

- "No, but the sacrifices of pagans are offered to demons, not to God, and I do not want you to be participants with demons" (1 Corinthians 10:20).
  - Warns us that participating in practices rooted in other deities is spiritually dangerous because they honor forces that are not from God.
- "But his delight is in the law of the LORD, and on his law he meditates day and night" (Psalm 1:2 ESV).
  - Reminds us that true meditation is delighting in God's Word and letting it guide our minds rather than emptying them.

Spiritual Self-Help and the Illusion of Mindfulness

I first got into self-help books around the same time I started doing yoga. I had just graduated college and was desperate for healing. After struggling with anxiety and depression for most of my life, these books felt like the answer I'd been waiting for. The idea of "mindfulness" was trending everywhere, and I genuinely believed that if I could just train my mind to stay present, I'd be healed. What I didn't realize then was that these kinds of spiritual self-help books and mindfulness practices have become normalized in our culture. They don't always look "New Age" on the surface. In fact, many business professionals, conservative families, or people who would never consider themselves spiritual at all can fall into them because the language sounds practical, harmless, even wise. But beneath the surface, the message is still the same deception: to look inward for salvation, instead of to God.

One of the first books I read was *The Power of Now* by Eckhart Tolle. The message was simple: Freedom from depression comes by surrendering to the moment. It sounded harmless, even helpful. But now I see that this ideology is dangerous because it replaces God with self. It tells people they can heal themselves, but only God can transform the mind and bring true peace. I have found that trying to heal myself only puts a huge weight on my shoulders that I wasn't meant to carry alone, and to be frank, couldn't. It only led to disappointment after disappointment and damage to me.

Books like *You Are a Badass* echoed the same message, only more boldly. The author constantly referred to "the Universe" instead of God and promoted the idea that truth is relative. She encouraged people to "take a leap of faith," "spend beyond your means," and trust that the universe would reward them. I actually believed this. I thought my financial struggles could be fixed by spending more money. I took a leap of faith and moved to LA, believing that if I acted like someone who was successful, the universe would catch me and make it happen. But that's not how truth works. That's not how God works. Only God provides. Only God sustains. And only God writes our story.

Self-help is appealing because it gives us the illusion of control. It tells us that we are enough, that the answers are within us, that we can fix ourselves if we just try hard enough. But that's not the gospel. The truth is, we are not enough on our own; we were never meant to be. We need a savior. And no self-help book can replace the healing and truth that comes through Jesus Christ.

Scripture to Expose the Deception:

- "Trust in the LORD with all your heart, and lean not on your own understanding" (Proverbs 3:5).
  - Self-help books often teach us to rely on our own wisdom, strength, and strategies, but Proverbs 3:5 warns us not to lean on our own understanding. Instead, true help and direction come from fully trusting the Lord.
- "Do not be conformed to this world, but be transformed by the renewal of your mind" (Romans 12:2 ESV).
  - Self-help focuses on conforming to worldly standards of success or happiness, but Romans 12:2 reminds us that true change comes only from God renewing our minds through his Spirit and truth.

Law of Attraction/Manifestation

Manifestation is the belief that your thoughts, energy, and intentions can shape your reality. It's often paired with the law of attraction, which teaches that "like attracts like." If you think positively and believe hard enough, you'll attract good things. It's also tied to something called creative visualization, where you imagine the life you want in vivid detail, such as your dream house, relationship, career, or body, and trust that the "universe" will deliver it if you match the right frequency or mindset.

On the surface, it sounds empowering. Who wouldn't want to believe that they can shape their future just by visualizing it or raising their vibration? It makes people feel like they're in control. That they're "co-creators with the universe." That they can manifest abundance, love, and success just by "aligning" with it.

But here's the issue: It's a lie that places you at the center of your own universe. Not only that, but it subtly pulls you away from the truth that God is the Creator and Author of life.

It boggles my mind how normalized and popular these ideas have become. People say things like "speak it into existence" or "I'm manifesting it" as if it's totally harmless. But I think it's gained so much popularity because there are *little* slivers of truth that people cling to. Maybe they wished to see dolphins and then actually did, or they made a vision board and later achieved some of those goals. Also, the Bible tells us there's power in the tongue, and what we speak and think truly does matter. But the devil knows Scripture too, and he twists that truth, turning it into something prideful and self-focused. Instead of giving glory to God, the focus becomes on *manifesting* our own desires, as if we hold the power rather than him. Manifestation is just a self-glorifying trap. It teaches you to believe that *you* are the source of all blessings and success. That your will is supreme. That your energy determines the outcome. But Scripture tells us the exact opposite: that God alone is sovereign, and his will—not ours—is what we should seek. Manifestation tells you to chase your own will. But Jesus teaches us to *surrender* ours and trust him instead. And the peace that comes from that surrender is something no vision board or frequency will ever give you.

Scripture to Expose the Deception:

- "You may say to yourself, 'My power and the strength of my hands have produced this wealth for me,' but remember the LORD your God, for it is he who gives you the ability to produce wealth . . ." (Deuteronomy 8:17–18).
  - Manifestation often encourages people to rely on their own "power" to create reality, but Deuteronomy 8:17–18 reminds us that true ability and provision come from God, not from ourselves or the universe.
- "Delight yourself in the LORD, and he will give you the desires of your heart" (Psalm 37:4 ESV).
  - Instead of trying to manifest what we want on our own, Psalm 37:4 reminds us to delight in God first. When our hearts align with him, he shapes and fulfills our true desires.

Karma and Reincarnation

Reincarnation is the belief that after you die, your soul is reborn into a new body, over and over again, until you've reached some kind of spiritual perfection or enlightenment. Karma is the idea that your actions (good or bad) follow you into your next life. So, if something terrible happens to you, it's seen as the result of bad karma from this life or a previous one. If good things happen, you're "reaping" your good deeds. It's all about cause and effect and earning your way to a better next life.

These beliefs are popular in Hinduism and Buddhism, and they are deeply embedded in New Age spirituality. People gravitate toward them because they explain suffering and promise second chances through endless lives, as if you get unlimited do-overs until you finally get it right.

I used to fully believe in this. I would look into my supposed past lives and try to draw meaning from them. I thought I must be on my "final life" because of all the revelations I was having and how spiritually mature I believed I was. I didn't realize at the time how prideful and deceiving that mindset was. But here's the truth: We don't get endless chances. The Bible says we live once, die once, and then face judgment. That may sound harsh to some, but it's actually merciful. Why? Because Jesus already paid the price. We don't have to spend lifetime after lifetime working off some invisible debt or hoping to be "good enough" in the next round. Jesus finished the work, and through Him, we get eternal life, not recycled ones.

Karma is also a distortion of God's justice. God is not a cosmic vending machine giving you what you "deserve." His grace is undeserved. His mercy doesn't follow the rules of karma; it breaks them entirely. The gospel is the good news that you *don't* get what your sins deserve, because Jesus took that punishment in your place. Reincarnation teaches that you must earn your way toward peace and perfection through endless striving. The gospel says Jesus did it once for all.

Scripture to Expose the Deception:

- "Just as people are destined to die once, and after that to face judgment . . . ." (Hebrews 9:27).
  - Karma and reincarnation suggest we live countless lives to work off our mistakes, but Hebrews 9:27 makes it clear that we die once and then face judgment. Our hope is not in cycles of rebirth but in Christ's gift of eternal life.
- "For the wages of sin is death, but the gift of God is eternal life in Christ Jesus our Lord" (Romans 6:23).
  - Karma teaches that we pay for our sins through endless cycles of cause and effect, but Romans 6:23 shows us the truth: The penalty for sin is death, and only through Jesus Christ do we receive the free gift of eternal life.

Astrology

What I didn't realize when I was in the middle of it is that astrology isn't just a distraction—it's actually dangerous. It brings you into agreement with spiritual forces that are *not* from God. Every time you read a horoscope or declare a personality trait based on your sign, you are unknowingly aligning with demonic influence. It's a form of counterfeit prophecy. Demons *do* study us. They *do* speak lies over our lives and attempt to curse us with confusion, fear, pride, and limitation. If you dig deep enough, you'll even find that certain zodiac signs are linked to different diseases, disorders, and mental patterns. On a more surface level, you'll see that astrology normalizes and excuses sin. "Oh, I'm just short-tempered because I'm an Aries," or "I'm flaky because I'm a Gemini," or "I'm controlling because I'm a Virgo." No, you're not bound to those traits. That's not your identity.

The Bible is very clear about astrology and divination. God calls it detestable, not because he wants to take away our fun, but because he wants to protect us. I didn't understand that I was centering my life around something that was never meant to guide me. The stars were created by God; they aren't meant to *replace* him.

Astrology gave me a false sense of control. But the truth is, the more I tried to rely on the stars, the more lost I became. I didn't need the universe to tell me who I was; I needed the Creator of the universe to redeem me. Once I started following Jesus, everything else lost its grip.

If you still check your horoscope "just for fun" or casually say, "I'm such a Cancer," or "It's because I'm a Taurus," I just want to lovingly warn you this is not harmless. Every time you speak those words, you're agreeing with a lie about your identity. You're giving the enemy permission to speak over your life. Even if it *feels* like it's working or giving you insight, it's coming from the wrong spirit. There's only one safe, true source of wisdom: God.

And let me tell you, what you choose to believe *has power* over your life. When I believed in astrology, I constantly saw "signs" that validated it. I felt sensitive to the full moons, the retrogrades, the zodiac seasons. But now I understand why. I was in agreement with it. I had *opened the door.* And when you come into agreement with lies, the enemy uses them to influence your thoughts, emotions, and even circumstances. But when I surrendered all of that to Jesus, when I renounced and rebuked it in his name, I was completely freed. I don't feel affected by moon phases or zodiac shifts anymore, not even a little bit. I don't engage with it, and because of that, it no longer has any grip on me. No part of my birth chart affects my life because I no longer give it permission to. I am no longer defined by the stars; I'm defined by the One who created them.

I am no longer defined by the stars; I'm defined by the One who created them.

Scripture to Expose the Deception:

- "Do not turn to mediums or seek out spiritists, for you will be defiled by them. I am the LORD your God" (Leviticus 19:31).
  - Astrology may seem harmless, but like mediums and spiritists, it seeks guidance from spiritual sources outside of God. Leviticus 19:31 warns that turning to these practices defiles us because only the Lord is meant to guide our lives.
- "And when you look up into the sky and see the sun, moon, and stars—all the forces of heaven—don't be seduced into worshiping them. The LORD your God gave them to all the peoples of the earth" (Deuteronomy 4:19 NLT).
  - Astrology tempts us to look to the sun, moon, and stars for direction, but Deuteronomy 4:19 warns us not to be seduced into worshiping or relying on them. They are part of God's creation, not sources of divine guidance.

Crystal Healing

Before I ever touched a tarot deck or pulled a manifestation card, I was already knee-deep in crystal healing. And honestly? It felt like a beautiful, natural thing. Who wouldn't be drawn to gorgeous, colorful rocks with "energy" that could align their chakras, clear their anxiety, protect them from negative vibes, or attract love, money, or peace?

I wasn't doing "magic" or spells (yet). I was just *setting intentions*. I cleansed my crystals in the moonlight. I placed them on my heart during meditation. I tucked them under my pillow for lucid dreams or peaceful sleep. I genuinely believed they were working, and I felt connected to something bigger. Something powerful.

And it wasn't just crystals. I burned sage and palo santo regularly to "clear the energy" in my home, cleanse my aura, and reset the vibe. It felt like a sacred ritual. I'd open the windows, set intentions, wave the smoke into each corner of the room, and believe I was pushing out negativity or evil. I didn't realize I was relying on objects to do what only God can truly do: protect, cleanse, and restore.

Let me be clear: I'm not saying that crystals don't carry a noticeable vibration. People definitely can feel something, and I certainly did. That's part of the allure, and part of the catch. If they didn't *do* something, no one would care. There's truth mixed in with the lie.

Different gems are said to have different qualities. You can assign different crystals to different "needs," set intentions with them, meditate with them, and *feel* a shift. But that doesn't make it good. Or safe. Or necessary. And when you step back and think about it, it's actually quite silly to believe a rock holds the power to heal your soul, cleanse your emotions, or protect you spiritually.

Crystals were created by God as part of his creation, not as tools to be idolized or used in rituals. Once we start assigning them power, we cross into spiritual territory. And any power that doesn't come from the Holy Spirit is not from the light, even if it *feels* good, calming, or beautiful.

Looking back, I see that crystals were a "safe" introduction to witchcraft. A soft entry into energy work, vibration obsession, and idolizing the universe instead of the Creator. It felt pure. But it wasn't. It was bait.

I didn't know it at the time, but I was already giving the enemy access to my life. I was coming into agreement with the idea that God wasn't enough, that I needed to add something extra to feel whole.

Scripture to Expose the Deception:

- "They exchanged the truth about God for a lie, and worshiped and served created things rather than the Creator—who is forever praised" (Romans 1:25).
  - Crystal healing places spiritual power in created objects rather than in the Creator himself, but Romans 1:25 reminds us that when we look to creation for healing or guidance, we trade the truth of God for a lie.
- "I am the LORD, who heals you" (Exodus 15:26).
  - Crystal healing claims that stones and minerals can restore us, but Exodus 15:26 makes it clear that true healing comes only from the Lord himself.

Psychedelics

Not everyone would lump psychedelics into New Age spirituality, but in my experience, they were deeply connected. Weed, mushrooms, acid, and ketamine weren't just "party drugs" or therapeutic tools. They were gateways into altered states of mind and paths leading into the spiritual realm.

Like many people, I smoked weed in high school a few times. I remember being shocked at how different it made me think. It felt like my brain got flipped inside out, and suddenly I noticed everything. After my spiritual awakening, I became more drawn to psychedelics. I started to see them as a *tool*. Something sacred. Something that could help me learn about myself and reality. I pushed through the fear and anxiety, thinking it was part of the "cleansing." But now I believe that anxiety was a warning. A signal that my spirit was under attack.

Because when you partake in these drugs, you're not just altering your state of mind. You're opening yourself up spiritually, allowing access to whatever wants to come in. And that "whatever" is not neutral. These altered states allow demonic spirits to whisper lies, offer counterfeits, and feed deception directly into your soul.

Acid intensified everything. It felt like time stopped, like I was tapping into a cosmic web of knowledge. But that was the danger, I was chasing wisdom without discernment. I believed I was having spiritual breakthroughs, but I was bypassing the Word of God entirely. I wasn't testing the spirits (1 John 4:1-3). I was accepting anything that felt deep, euphoric, or mystical.

I believed the mushroom trips were healing me. I told myself this was "shadow work," that I was facing my pain to build myself back up. I thought I was brave. I thought I was *evolving*. But here's the truth: God never asked me to do that. He didn't call me to access the truth through psychedelic portals. He didn't call me to break myself down through spiritual drugs. He called me to come to him, to receive freedom through his Spirit, not through altered ones.

The Bible says, "Be alert and of sober mind. Your enemy the devil prowls around like a roaring lion looking for someone to devour" (1 Peter 5:8). It means what it says. It's not just about avoiding drunkenness; it's about guarding your mind from openings that allow spiritual intrusion. The Greek word *pharmakeia* (from which we get "pharmacy") is used in Galatians 5:20 to describe sorcery, and it refers to the use of drugs for spiritual and magical practices. It's not a stretch to see the connection.

Especially now, psychedelics are becoming wildly mainstream. They're being marketed as therapy. As medicine. As a fast track to healing trauma, finding inner peace, or even "meeting God." But what people are really chasing is spiritual fruit without spiritual roots, healing without repentance, enlightenment without the Holy Spirit, revelation without relationship.

Even the way these substances work—by disrupting serotonin, suppressing the default mode network, and increasing suggestibility—makes the brain vulnerable to manipulation. In those moments, you're open to anything. And "anything" can be dangerous.

If you're dabbling in psychedelics, whether it's for fun, curiosity, healing, or "spiritual growth," you are opening a door. And what walks through that door is not neutral, no matter how euphoric or insightful it may feel. These substances offer a false light, a counterfeit revelation. But they will never lead you to truth, peace, or salvation. Only Jesus can do that.

The only One worth surrendering your mind to is the One who created it.

And if you've already walked this road, if you've experimented, opened doors, and believed the lies, you can still close those doors. Right now. Repent, renounce, and give it all to God. He is faithful to forgive, cleanse, and protect you. That's what he did for me. He took my chaos, my deception, and my counterfeit spirituality and replaced it with freedom, clarity, and peace. The real kind. The lasting kind.

You don't need altered states to wake up. You need the Holy Spirit to be born again.

> You don't need altered states to wake up. You need the Holy Spirit to be born again.

Scripture to Expose the Deception:

- "Therefore, preparing your minds for action, and being sober-minded, set your hope fully on the grace that will be brought to you at the revelation of Jesus Christ" (1 Peter 1:13 ESV).
  - Psychedelics promise spiritual insight by altering the mind, but 1 Peter 1:13 calls us to be sober-minded and to set our hope not on altered states, but on the grace and truth revealed in Jesus Christ.
- "The acts of the flesh are obvious: sexual immorality, impurity and debauchery; idolatry and witchcraft . . . I warn you, as I did before, that those who live like this will not inherit the kingdom of God" (Galatians 5:19–21).
  - The Bible is clear that using substances to alter our minds and open spiritual doors is a form of witchcraft (*pharmakeia*), and Galatians 5:19–21 warns that those who practice such things will not inherit the kingdom of God.

Witchcraft/Tarot Cards/Psychics

Witchcraft

At its core, witchcraft refers to the use of supernatural or spiritual powers to influence the natural world. Historically, it has involved rituals, spells, charms, divination, and communication with spirits. While mainstream media now often portrays witches as quirky, empowered, or misunderstood women, the roots of witchcraft are deeply spiritual, and not in a holy way. It stems from pagan and occult traditions that seek hidden knowledge and power apart from God. The Bible is crystal clear: Any form of witchcraft, sorcery, or divination is detestable to the Lord (see Deuteronomy 18:10–12). What the world romanticizes, God warns us to run from.

Could this be the most dangerous and most obviously evil practice hidden in plain sight? I thought I had been deceived about witches being "bad." I was duped into thinking that witches were misunderstood healers, burned at the stake because others were jealous and intimidated by their feminine powers. I began to embrace a false sense of empowerment tied to my womanhood. It all sounded great to a woman in victimhood looking for vengeance and control, but was that the truth?

This narrative is easily spread in New Age shops, feminist circles, and popular media. It seems harmless at first. I picked up a book on witchcraft, and I was hooked. I began to believe that witchcraft held the key to who I truly was. I started collecting things. A mini cauldron for manifestation spells. A crystal ball for the aesthetic but also for what it represented. I got more piercings, more tattoos. Before I knew it, I was fully embracing the identity of a witch. I claimed it proudly, without giving much thought to what I was really aligning myself with.

There are many types of witchcraft, such as Wiccan, cosmic, lightworker, kitchen, shadow, and more. I gravitated toward "Green Witch" practices, focused on nature and herbs. That's when I bought my first tarot deck: *The Green Witch Tarot.*

Tarot Cards

Tarot is a form of divination, a practice used to gain hidden knowledge or insight through spiritual means. Tarot decks typically contain seventy-eight cards, each with symbolic meanings. The cards are often used in specific layouts (called spreads) to answer questions about the past, present, or future. While many believe tarot taps into intuition or "universal energy," it's really another form of occult communication, often opening people up to deceiving spirits. It may seem innocent or aesthetic at first, but it's a spiritual tool that invites the wrong kind of power into your life. God's Word warns us not to seek knowledge from the spiritual realm outside of him—because there are real spirits behind it, and not the kind you want around.

There are many ways to read tarot. Some people follow traditional spreads while others do intuitive readings. Either way, the idea is that the cards reveal what has happened, what's happening now, and what's coming next.

I got hooked quickly. My readings seemed to *predict* major events in my life, like the *Death* card showing up just before Cody and I broke up or *The Tower* card right before I was fired from my job. It felt like gambling with fate.

Out of all the New Age practices I engaged in, tarot felt the most twisted. It scared me. I didn't know what the cards would say each time I pulled them, and yet, I gave them power. They had a strange, spiritual grip on me, like I was handing over control of my life to something unseen.

Psychics

Psychics claim to have special abilities to see the future, speak with the dead, or reveal hidden knowledge about your life. They often use tools like tarot cards, palm readings, crystal balls, or "spirit guides" to deliver their messages.

It may seem like psychics have a special gift. I have found myself wondering, "How did she know that?" In reality, they are misusing that gift to prey on the vulnerable and the lost. Many communicate with dark spirits, which may already be lurking in your life, gathering information about you and keeping you in spiritual bondage.

At first, a psychic's help may feel comforting. Who doesn't want answers about the future or to hear from a loved one who has passed away? But the Bible is clear that seeking guidance from psychics is forbidden (Deuteronomy 18:10–12, Isaiah 8:19). These practices open the door to deception and spiritual oppression.

God never intended for us to seek secret knowledge apart from him. True peace and direction come from the Holy Spirit and God's Word, not from those claiming to see beyond the veil. What psychics offer is a counterfeit. Satan has always tried to imitate God's power, but it only leads to confusion and destruction. Jesus is the only one who truly knows the future, and he calls us to trust him, not human "mediums."

Scripture to Expose the Deception:

- "Let no one be found among you who sacrifices their son or daughter in the fire, who practices divination, interprets omens, practices witchcraft, or casts spells, or who is a medium or spiritist or who consults the dead. Anyone who does these things is detestable to the LORD, and because of these detestable practices the LORD your God will drive out those nations before you" (Deuteronomy 18:10–12).
  - Practices like consulting psychics, reading tarot, or engaging in witchcraft fall squarely under the detestable actions listed in Deuteronomy 18:10–12. God warns that these activities are not harmless. They are spiritually dangerous and opposed to his will.
- "When someone tells you to consult mediums and spiritists, who whisper and mutter, should not a people inquire of their God? Why consult the dead on behalf of the living?" (Isaiah 8:19)
  - Rather than turning to psychics, tarot readers, or spiritists for guidance, Isaiah 8:19 reminds us that we should consult God himself. He alone knows our lives and has the authority to guide us.

Chakras and Reiki

Chakras are believed to be energy centers within the body, according to ancient Eastern traditions, particularly from Hinduism and Buddhism. There are seven main chakras, each associated with a different aspect of physical, emotional, and spiritual well-being. The idea is that if your chakras are "blocked" or "unbalanced," then your life will be out of alignment, leading to issues in everything from health to relationships to career and even to your spiritual growth. In my time in the New Age, I believed that if I didn't keep my chakras perfectly aligned, my life would fall apart. I was consumed with the idea of balancing them to achieve peace and success.

I didn't realize that these teachings were rooted in occult spirituality, and they would subtly shift my focus from God and his plan for me to my own self-centered pursuit of "balance" and "empowerment."

The Bible doesn't mention chakras, but it does speak against practices that open doors to spiritual deception (Deuteronomy 18:10–12). The concept of energy centers, along with the rituals that often accompany chakra work, is demonic. It invites forces that are not of God into your life under the guise of healing and personal growth.

Scripture to Expose the Deception:

- "See to it that no one takes you captive through hollow and deceptive philosophy, which depends on human tradition and the elemental spiritual forces of this world rather than on Christ" (Colossians 2:8).

· Chakras and energy healing often teach that spiritual power flows through the body and can be manipulated, but Colossians 2:8 warns that relying on these "forces" apart from Christ is deceptive and leads us away from God's truth.

Synchronicity and Angel Numbers

Synchronicity, a term coined by famous Swiss psychologist Carl Jung, refers to the belief that meaningful coincidences occur when events align in ways that seem more than just random. In the New Age, synchronicity is often viewed as the universe trying to send you a message, guiding your path with signs that validate your choices and feelings. For a time, I was completely immersed in this belief. I started seeing "signs" everywhere. In license plates, on road signs, in pamphlets handed to me by strangers, and especially in repeating numbers. I believed these were messages from the universe confirming that I was on the right path.

I started fixating on Angel Numbers, which are specific, re-petitive number sequences like 111, 222, 333, or even 666, said to be spiritual messages guiding your life. I would see numbers like 11:11 on the clock or 333 on a random street sign, and I believed these were signs meant to guide me toward something important. Every time I saw them, I'd feel like I was being directed by some higher power, and I'd eagerly look up their meanings in books or online. But the more I searched for meaning in these numbers, the more I felt lost. It was as if I was trapped in a never-ending cycle of seeking answers that never came.

What I didn't realize then was that these "signs" were not divine messages. They were distractions, leading me further away from the truth. Rather than offering peace or clarity, they pulled me deeper into confusion. The Bible warns against seeking after signs and wonders because they can lead to spiritual deception (Matthew 12:39). Instead of helping me, these signs kept me trapped in a false spiritual world.

I also now understand that the whole idea of synchronicity, especially when it comes to Angel Numbers, is rooted in New Age thinking and can be dangerous. It redirects your attention from seeking God's truth to chasing after illusions and empty promises. The obsession with seeing signs in everything is an invitation to be led astray. These distractions only served to keep me focused on anything but the true source of guidance, which is God's Word.

Scripture to Expose the Deception:

- "The heart of man plans his way, but the Lord establishes his steps" (Proverbs 16:9 ESV).
  - Synchronicities and Angel Numbers may seem like divine guidance, but Proverbs 16:9 reminds us that it is God, not arbitrary signs or patterns, who truly directs our steps.

Shadow Work and Inner Child Healing

In New Age practices, the idea of shadow work involves confronting and integrating your so-called "shadow self." The shadow self, according to New Age teachings, is made up of all the dark, repressed parts of your personality—those things you're ashamed of or that you've been taught are "bad." The goal of shadow work is to accept and embrace these parts of yourself, giving them power and control in your life.

It sounds somewhat empowering at first to accept your "dark side," right? But here's the problem: Embracing your sin and darkness does not lead to healing. It leads to further spiritual deception. The Bible calls us to live in the light, not to cozy up to our darkness. Ephesians 5:8–11 tells us, "For you were once darkness, but now you are light in the Lord. Live as children of light . . . Have nothing to do with the fruitless deeds of darkness, but rather expose them." God doesn't want us to integrate our shadows; he calls us to cast off the works of darkness and be transformed by his light.

Similarly, the concept of inner child healing is another New Age idea that gained traction in spiritual circles. It's the belief that in order to heal, we must reconnect with our "inner child"—the version of ourselves that was hurt, abused, or traumatized—and nurture and re-parent that child. The idea is that if we confront these old wounds, we can heal and reclaim our power.

While it's true that childhood trauma can affect us, the Bible doesn't tell us to "heal our inner child." It tells us to bring our burdens and pain to Jesus, who can heal our hearts and souls. Matthew 11:28-30 invites us, "Come to me, all you who are weary and burdened, and I will give you rest . . . For my yoke is easy and my burden is light." Jesus doesn't require us to dive into our past darkness; he offers a way out of it through him.

We're not called to live in our brokenness; we're called to be healed and transformed by God's grace.

Both of these New Age practices are attempts to validate sin and darkness. In in reality, what we need to do is to turn to the light of Christ for healing and freedom. We're not called to live in our brokenness; we're called to be healed and transformed by God's grace.

Scripture to Expose the Deception:

- "He heals the brokenhearted and binds up their wounds" (Psalm 147:3).
  - Inner child work and shadow work often encourage us to heal ourselves or confront our past in our own strength, but Psalm 147:3 reminds us that true healing comes from God, who binds up our wounds and restores our hearts.

Conclusion

The New Age offers many enticing practices and beliefs that promise healing, empowerment, and spiritual growth. However, behind these appealing ideas lies a dangerous deception. Each of the concepts—whether it's tarot, witchcraft, twin flames, or shadow work—may seem innocent or even spiritually fulfilling, but they ultimately lead us away from the truth of God and his plan for our lives.

These practices, rooted in ancient paganism, mysticism, and occultism, try to fill a God-shaped void with counterfeit spirituality. They make us look inward, focus on self, and embrace darkness rather than turning to the light of Christ. The enemy uses these tools to distract us from the healing and transformation that comes from a relationship with Jesus.

If anything, these practices place a crushing weight of responsibility on you, making you feel like the one responsible for your healing, your growth, and your life's direction. If you've been deeply wounded, that burden can be overwhelming. The truth is, healing isn't something we can do on our own. Surrendering to God is the greatest relief you can experience. When you place your trust in him, he takes the weight off your shoulders and shows you that he can move mountains far more efficiently than you ever could. The peace that comes from surrendering to God is something the New Age can never offer.

Again, my hope in sharing this personal glossary of New Age terms is not to condemn but to equip you with the knowledge to recognize these lies. I lived in this deception for a long time, and I know how easy it is to get swept up in the allure of self-empowerment and spiritual awakening. But the truth is that real healing, peace, and purpose are found in Christ alone. As you reflect on these practices, I encourage you to compare them

You don't have to settle for a counterfeit version of spirituality. Jesus offers you the real thing.

to what God's Word says. The truth of the Bible stands in stark contrast to the empty promises of the New Age. You don't have to settle for a counterfeit version of spirituality. Jesus offers you the real thing.

APPENDIX B

WHY JESUS, WHY NOW?

Have you ever wondered why we measure time the way we do? Why the year is 2025 and what exactly happened 2,025 years ago to mark the divide between "before" and "after"? The very framework of time itself is centered around one man: Jesus Christ. Even if you don't believe in him, history does.

If Jesus isn't real, then why is his life the dividing line of human history? Why is his birthday the most widely celebrated holiday in the world? Why is it that believers and non-believers alike can't seem to stop saying his name, whether in praise or in profanity? His name carries weight, even among those who deny him. And where did the idea come from to have courtroom witnesses swear to tell the truth with their hand on a Bible?

Despite his undeniable influence, so many people—me included—have rejected the Bible without ever truly reading it. We dismiss it, we critique it, we claim to know what it says, yet we've never taken the time to open it for ourselves, or we take verses out of context without taking the time to understand it. But here's what I've learned: When you stop and seek the truth, when you learn the story of creation and the gospel of Jesus Christ, everything in this world starts to make sense.

From Atheism to Awakening

For most of my life, I didn't believe in anything I couldn't see or touch. I grew up believing that science had all the answers and that the Bible was nothing more than a collection of outdated myths.

As I got older, I embraced atheism completely—not just as a belief, but as an identity. Atheism made me feel intelligent. The more I understood evolution, the Big Bang, and the complexities of the universe, the smarter I felt. I saw Christians as ignorant, people who needed fairy tales to cope with life. I, on the other hand, had *logic* on my side. My knowledge gave me a sense of superiority and pride in knowing I had things figured out.

Atheism also carried a strange kind of comfort. If we were just floating on a rock, spinning through an infinite, indifferent universe, then nothing really mattered. Life had no deeper meaning, no ultimate consequences. But the idea of a God who created me, saw everything I did, and had a purpose for my life? That felt suffocating. Given the weight of my childhood traumas and the suffering I had witnessed, the idea of a loving God seemed impossible. If he existed, why had he allowed so much pain? It was easier to believe he wasn't there at all.

But despite my confidence in science, a quiet unease lingered in the back of my mind. The more I studied, the more I began to question. *Where did all this come from? How did it all begin?* No matter how deep I dug, I couldn't escape the realization that something was missing.

I rejected God, but I couldn't ignore the overwhelming complexity, order, and beauty of the universe. The intricate design of life, the way everything seemed to operate with precise intention, the complexities of the human brain and the emotions we feel, consciousness, and an almost inherent knowledge of right from wrong. It all left me unsettled. Science alone couldn't even begin to answer everything.

That's when the cracks in my atheism began to form. I had spent years dismissing anything beyond the physical world, but now, I wasn't so sure. My understanding of the universe was beginning to unravel, and I found myself searching for answers in places I never thought I would.

Living in a Spiritual World

My depression had already convinced me that life had no real meaning, but my spiritual awakening through yoga changed that. For the first time, I knew without a doubt that the spiritual realm was real. What I didn't realize at the time was that not everything spiritual is good.

I had no fear of the true God. In hindsight, I see that I was still clinging to anger and bitterness toward him because of the pain I had endured. I wanted to be "open" to everything, to be a free spirit, to seek truth on my own terms. But being open to everything makes you susceptible to deception. And deception, especially when it masquerades as enlightenment, only leads you further from the truth.

I was experiencing real spiritual encounters, but I lacked discernment. I had entered a world of possibilities without questioning what was actually *true*. Even though I felt transformed in some ways, I didn't yet understand the deeper realities of sin, separation, and the need for redemption. The spiritual realm was alive, but it wasn't necessarily good. And that left me with a crucial question: If everything is spiritual, then what is the ultimate truth?

This journey would eventually lead me to confront the root of our brokenness, which is the reality of sin.

The Beginning: Sin and Separation

I didn't grow up hearing Bible stories at bedtime, but I remember the first time I really heard the story of Adam and Eve and actually *understood* it. It was more than just a tale about a forbidden fruit. It hit me that what happened in the garden wasn't about a snack gone wrong. It was about trust. About humans deciding they knew better than God. That moment of rebellion didn't just bring consequences; it introduced separation, suffering, and a ripple effect we still feel today.

What really stood out to me was that God allowed it. Not because he's cruel or distant, but because love has to be chosen. He didn't force himself on anyone; he gave humanity the dignity of free will. But with that came the risk that we'd use it to walk away. And we did. Over and over again. The more I read the Bible, the more I saw myself in that pattern—wanting control, defining truth on my own terms, and chasing success, approval, relationships, or anything to fill a God-sized gap.

As humanity spread across the earth, we forgot God and replaced him with something less. In the Old Testament, people built golden idols, worshiped false gods, and followed their own desires. Over and over, God sent warnings through prophets, yet people kept turning away.

Today, we do the same thing. We call our idols something else, though. Instead of golden statues, we worship the universe, manifestation, crystals, self-enlightenment. Instead of ancient rituals, we follow horoscopes, psychics, and energy healing. The deception is the same but wears a different mask.

But idolatry isn't always obvious. We may think it's about bowing to a statue, but it's also about what we trust, seek, and devote ourselves to. Anything that takes God's place in our hearts becomes an idol. Whether it's money, success, relationships, or even our own desires, when we put anything above God, we fall into the same trap humanity has for thousands of years.

And where does this leave us? The consequence of idolatry, and all sin, is separation from God. And because God is just, he cannot overlook it. The price of sin has always been death. Yet from the very beginning, God had a plan to redeem us.

God's Justice and the Price of Sin

If God is truly just, he can't ignore sin. A judge who lets criminals walk free wouldn't be a good judge, and God is the ultimate judge. The price of sin is death, which means not just physical death but eternal separation from God. That's why, in the Old Testament, sacrifices were required. Blood had to be shed to cover sin. But those sacrifices were only temporary, a foreshadowing of something greater.

Yet, God's justice is not the end of the story. The price had to be paid, but in his mercy, God chose to pay it himself. Jesus, God in human form, came to take on our sin and bear the punishment we rightfully deserved. His sacrifice wasn't another temporary covering but the ultimate fulfillment of God's justice. Through Jesus alone, we can be restored to a right relationship with God.

The only way to fix what was broken was for God himself to step in. And he did. Jesus came to take on our punishment, to fulfill the law, to become the final sacrifice. He lived a perfect, sinless life—something none of us can ever do. And then he willingly took all our sin, all our punishment, and paid the price with his own blood.

It was finished. No more sacrifices. No more separation. Through Jesus, we can be restored to God, not by our own efforts, but by what he did for us. That's why no other path leads to salvation. No amount of good works, self-discovery, or positive energy can erase sin. Only Jesus can do that. And he did.

The Dismissal of Faith: More Than Just a Difference in Beliefs

One thing I've learned over the years is that just because someone doesn't believe in God doesn't mean their arguments are automatically true. Too often, atheists and skeptics resort to mockery, dismissing Christians as "naïve" or "too stupid to understand the evidence." They claim science has proven there is no God, yet their approach often involves shutting down opposing viewpoints rather than engaging with the facts. This tactic of dismissal is intellectually dishonest and reveals something deeper: a refusal to consider that faith might actually hold real answers.

Dismissing someone's belief doesn't make the truth disappear. It simply reveals a lack of understanding on the denier's part, or perhaps a fear of the consequences of sin. It's easy to label someone as wrong when you refuse to hear their case. But in my experience, the scientific and historical evidence for the existence of God—and for Jesus Christ—is often deliberately ignored or misrepresented.

The Influence of the World: Education, Media, and Government

It's important to recognize that those who reject God often have the full weight of the education system, media, and even government behind them. These institutions, which shape much of our society's worldview, are dominated by secular ideologies that marginalize or ridicule the Christian faith. From the textbooks we read to the movies we watch, and even the policies that govern our lives, many of the ideas we are taught reinforce the narrative that God doesn't exist, and that faith is either foolish or naïve.

In reality, it's hard to deny that we live in a world that has been heavily influenced by forces actively working to deceive us and keep us from the truth. The Bible speaks to this directly. In 2 Corinthians 4:4, Paul refers to Satan as the "god of this age" who blinds the minds of unbelievers, preventing them from seeing the light of the gospel of Christ. These forces have used every avenue available to twist the truth and prevent people from recognizing the reality of God's power and truth. However, Romans 1:20 confirms that there is no excuse for someone to not believe in God: "For ever since the world was created, people have seen the earth and sky. Through everything God made, they can clearly see his invisible qualities—his eternal power and divine nature. So they have no excuse for not knowing God" (NLT).

When we consider how pervasive these secular forces are in society, it's no wonder that many people struggle to see the evidence of God. The narrative is controlled by those who deny his existence. The media only presents one side of the argument, and the public education system teaches evolution as fact without presenting alternative viewpoints. This makes it increasingly difficult for people to even consider the possibility that God exists, let alone accept that Jesus Christ is the truth.

But this is precisely what the Bible warned us about. In Ephesians 6:12, Paul writes that "our struggle is not against flesh and blood, but against the rulers, against the authorities, against the powers of this dark world and against the spiritual forces of evil in the heavenly realms." The battle is both intellectual and spiritual. Satan has shaped the world to dismiss the truth of God's Word. The systems we rely on are broken and fallen, and they often operate under the influence of powers opposed to God.

As followers of Christ, we are called to be a light in a dark world, to stand firm in the truth of God's Word, even when it's unpopular or countercultural. But we must also understand that the systems of this world are not neutral. They are part of a larger spiritual battle that is unfolding before us. Knowing this should strengthen our resolve to seek the truth, to stand firm in our faith, and to share the gospel with others. The truth is not only something we grasp with our minds, but it is also something we must fight for in the spiritual realm.

The Big Bang vs. the Laws of Thermodynamics

The Big Bang theory raises serious questions when compared to two of the most established scientific laws: the First and Second Laws of Thermodynamics. The First Law says that energy can't be created or destroyed, only transformed, yet the Big Bang claims everything came from nothing. Even scientists admit they don't have a clear explanation. If energy and matter can't simply appear, then something outside the system must have created it. That something, many of us believe, is God.

The Second Law states that everything naturally moves from order to disorder, not the other way around. But the Big Bang suggests a chaotic explosion somehow produced galaxies, life, and human intelligence. How can an explosion bring about such intricate design when explosions usually destroy? Evolutionary explanations rely on randomness and time, but this still goes against the natural tendency of things to break down instead of becoming more complex. The order we see in the universe points to a Creator, not chaos.

Propaganda and Programing

Of course, there are plenty of other gaps, contradictions, and propaganda surrounding mainstream science that many re- searchers and independent thinkers have pointed out. From the inconsistencies in radiometric dating to the impossibility of life forming from non-life, the list goes on. But for me, I don't even need to go that far. The contradictions between the Big Bang and the fundamental laws of physics are enough to tell me that something isn't adding up. And when you really think about it, most of what we believe about the universe was drilled into us from the moment we entered the education system, a system that, let's be honest, is not designed to encourage critical thinking but to condition us into a particular worldview. We've been taught to accept these theories as fact from such a young age that we never even stopped to question them. But now, as adults, we have a responsibility to do exactly that. What if we've been lied to? What if the truth was there all along, but we were too blinded by what we were taught to see it?

The Only Explanation That Makes Sense

The truth is, the universe had to come from something outside the natural world, something that is not bound by time, space, or material existence. And the only explanation that fits both logic and science is that the universe was intentionally designed by a Creator. The Bible describes God as eternal, meaning he exists outside of time and is not bound by physical laws. He is the only possible answer to the mystery of our origins.

The deeper you dig, the more you realize that it takes far more faith to believe in the Big Bang than it does to believe in God.

It's incredible that when you break free from the mainstream narrative and truly examine the evidence, all of it points directly to God. The very things dismissed as outdated or "anti-science" actually hold more truth than the ever-changing theories the world clings to. But it doesn't stop there. Science alone isn't what

> The deeper you dig, the more you realize that it takes far more faith to believe in the Big Bang than it does to believe in God.

convinced me. What sealed it was the Bible itself.

Everything happening in the world today is exactly what the living Word of God foretold. The normalization of sin, the rebellion against God's design, and the outright hatred for Jesus and his followers—it's all written in Scripture.

The Bible warns that in the last days, people would turn away from truth and embrace deception: "For the time will come when people will not put up with sound doctrine. Instead, to suit their own desires, they will gather around them a great number of teachers to say what their itching ears want to hear" (2 Timothy 4:3).

We see this happening right now. Society celebrates what God calls sin, twisting morality into something subjective rather than absolute. Homosexuality and transgenderism are aggressively promoted, while those who stand for biblical truth are silenced, ridiculed, or even persecuted:

- "You shall not lie with a male as with a woman; it is an abomination" (Leviticus 18:22 ESV).
- "Therefore God gave them up in the lusts of their hearts to impurity, to the dishonoring of their bodies among themselves" (Romans 1:24 ESV).
- "Woe to those who call evil good and good evil, who put darkness for light and light for darkness" (Isaiah 5:20).

Jesus himself warned that the world would hate those who follow him:

- "If the world hates you, keep in mind that it hated me first" (John 15:18).
- "Indeed, all who desire to live a godly life in Christ Jesus will be persecuted" (2 Timothy 3:12 ESV).

It's no coincidence that biblical values are being attacked while sin is glorified. This is spiritual warfare. The devil has infiltrated the education system, the media, and the government, pushing a godless agenda while trying to silence anything that points to the truth of Jesus Christ. But no matter how much the world tries to erase him, the truth remains.

The Bible predicted all of this, proving once again that it isn't just an old religious book but the living, breathing Word of God.

The Personal Truth of Following Jesus

It's one thing to study evidence, to recognize the flaws in modern theories, and to see how the Bible aligns with what's happening in the world today. But even with all of that, nothing compares to experiencing the truth of Jesus firsthand. I can't deny what he has done in my life. No one can take away the transformation I've gone through since surrendering to him.

And as I walked in obedience, I saw the fruit of that surrender. Doors that had once been shut swung open. Relationships were restored. My purpose became clearer. The chaos that once ruled my life was replaced with stability, direction, and a confidence that came not from myself, but from knowing that God was in control.

The Bible says, "You will know them by their fruits" (Matthew 7:16 NASB). When you follow Jesus, your life bears fruit. It doesn't mean everything is easy or perfect, but it means you are no longer fighting alone. Healing, restoration, and blessings follow obedience.

And when you truly experience Jesus, when you feel the weight of sin lifted and the power of his love, you can't go back.

The best part? This isn't just for me. It's for *you*, too. God is always near, always ready to welcome you into His arms. "Draw near to God, and he will draw near to you" (James 4:8 ESV). His love is freely given. He's waiting for you to choose him. "For God so loved the world that he gave his only Son, that whoever believes in him should not perish but have eternal life" (John 3:16 ESV). He has given us free will, the ability to make our own choices, but the truth is, there is only *one* way to eternal life and that is through Jesus Christ. "I am the way and the truth and the life. No one comes to the Father except through me" (John 14:6).

If any of this resonates with you, if you have been searching, longing for something real, something that actually brings peace, then there is only *one* way to find it. The only One who can provide it for you is Jesus.

ACKNOWLEDGMENTS

First and foremost, I give all glory to God, who forgave me so I could move forward, who pulled me out of darkness and gave me a new life in Jesus Christ. Without him, this book would not exist, and neither would I.

To my husband, Josiah, thank you for standing by me, believing in me, and walking with me through the mess and the miracle. Your love, patience, and support made this possible.

To my daughter, Aurora, you are my greatest earthly blessing and the reason I fight to live in truth every day.

To my Nana and Papa, for taking me in, mentoring and discipling me, and showing me the love, peace, and fruitfulness of living in faith. You have always been patient and prayerful toward me and given me grace.

To my mom, who never left my side, even while juggling ten kids and navigating through a hard situation. Thank you for letting me vent and helping me so I did not carry all this alone. God is working in our family to heal and restore, and I can't wait for you to share your story of redemption one day too.

To my family and friends who have prayed for me, encouraged me, and reminded me that God's grace is bigger than my failures. I am forever grateful.

To my church family and mentors who poured into me as I stumbled forward in faith. Thank you for your wisdom, your prayers, and your example of Christlike love.

To my writing coach, Traci Matt, who believed in this message even when I doubted myself. Thank you for helping me give shape to the story God wrote in my life.

To my publishing team, thank you for helping me bring this story to the world with excellence and care.

Finally, to the reader holding this book, thank you for opening your heart and letting me share my story with you. My prayer is that through these pages, you see not me, but Jesus, the One who redeems, restores, and makes all things new.

ABOUT THE AUTHOR

Once trapped in New Age deception and a broken past, Abigail Myatt was radically transformed by the saving grace of Jesus Christ. Now a wife, mother, and writer, she is passionate about helping others break free from the lies of the world and discover the truth, freedom, and hope found only in him. Abigail shares her testimony and encouragement through writing, speaking, and online ministry. She lives in Ohio with her husband and daughter.

HELP SHARE THE MESSAGE

Dear Reader,

Thank you so much for joining me on this journey of faith and transformation! If this book has touched your heart, I'd be so grateful if you could leave an honest review on Amazon. Your feedback not only encourages me but also helps others discover this message of hope and redemption.

Every review you leave plays a crucial role in spreading the light of the gospel to more people who need it. Your support truly makes a difference.

Thank you for being a part of this journey and for sharing the message with others.

With gratitude,
Abigail